WOMEN EDUCATION

THE AUTHOR

Jogesh Chandra Pati (*b*. 1952) obtained his M. Sc. in Zoology (1974) from Utkal University Vani Vihar, Bhubaneswar and MEd from Regional College of Education, Bhubaneswar (1977). He has completed many Research Projects sponsored by U.G.C., Kolkata. His areas of research interest are Entomology, Measurement, Evaluation and Guidance, Educational Psychology, Micro Teaching and Tribal Education. He has been working as Lecturer from 1975 in different institutions of repute of Orissa. e.g. Regional College of Education, Bhubaneswar, Hindusthan Aeronautics College, Sunabedha, Koraput, D. K. College, Jaleswar, Balasore, S.V.M. College, Jagatsinghpur. At present he is acting as Principal, U.N.S. Mahavidyalaya, Khairabad, Mugpal, Jajpur affiliated to Utkal University, Vani Vihar, Bhubaneswar, Orissa.

Rajan Kumar Sahoo (*b*. 1961) obtained his M.A. in Economics (1984) from Ravenshaw College, Cuttack and LL.B. from M. S. Law College, Cuttack in 1994. He was awarded Ph.D degree in the year 2000 from Utkal University, Vani Vihar, Bhubaneswar (Orissa). He has published 62 papers and 95 articles in different newspapers, magazines, journals and books. He has completed many Research Projects and organised both national and state level Conferences and Seminars on Economics sponsored by U.G.C., Kolkata. His important works are Tribal Development in India, Co-operatives for Economic Development. Besides this he has jointly edited books like *Self-Help Groups and Women Empowerment*, and *Regional Rural Banks and Agricultural Development*. His areas of research interest are Banking and Monetary Management, Tribal Development Co-operative Movement, Agricultural Marketing Resource Economics and Women Studies. He has been working as Lecturer in Economics since 1985. At present he is in U.N.S. Mahavidyalaya, Khairabad, Mugpal, Jajpur, affiliated to Utkal University, Vani Vihar, Bhubaneswar, Orissa.

Hari Ballav Dash (*b*. 1960) obtained his M.A. in Education (1984) and M.Phil in Education (1985) from Kurukshetra University, Haryana. He has organised national level Conferences on Education sponsored by U.G.C., Kolkata. His areas of research interest are Educational Psychology, Educational Technology, Women's Education and Sex Education. He has been working as Lecturer in Education since 1986. At present he is in U.N.S. Mahavidyalaya, Khairabad, Mugpal, Jajpur, affiliated to Utkal University, Vani Vihar, Bhubaneswar, Orissa.

WOMEN EDUCATION

—Emerging Issues and Rethinking

Edited by

JOGESH CHANDRA PATI
RAJAN KUMAR SAHOO
HARIBALLAV DASH

MITTAL PUBLICATIONS
NEW DELHI (INDIA)

First Published 2008

ISBN 81-8324-260-X

Published and printed by Krishan Mittal for Mittal Publications,
4594/9, Daryaganj, New Delhi - 110002, India.
Phone: 23250398, 25351493 ***Telefax***: 91-11-25351521
e-mail : mittalp@ndf.vsnl.net.in
Website : www.mittalbooks.com

PREFACE

Women constitute an important segment of society and comprise nearly fifty percent of the population. They perform multiple roles as mothers, housewives and wage earners. They are the agents of change. They contribute 2/3rd of the world's work hours, earn only 1/3rd of the total income and own less that 1/10th of the world resources. Their literates constitute 44.5 per cent of total literates, their per cent at ministerial level is 10 per cent and at economic activity level is 42.

Education is essential to enable them to participate and benefit from the development process. It can help them to enhance their literacy skills, better hygiene, caring for family health, utilization of leisure time to develop the vocational skills for their economic enhancement to fight against exploitation and to conquer the disadvantage and discrimination which they suffer from. There is a positive co-relation between women literacy rate and life expectancy.

On the other hand illiteracy is associated with poverty, malnutrition, deprivation, high mortality, high population growth and other aspects of under development. Lack of education, training and low level of literacy excludes women from social, economic, political as well as knowledge power. As a consequence of which in political horizon out of 27,50,865 elected Gram Panchayat members in India, their number is 5,77,270. Out of 1,48,697 elected panchayat samiti members and 12,516 members in Zilla Parisads, they occupy only 37,611 and 2,993 respectively. Hence women education is imperative.

Since independence various Commissions and Committees have recommended for the development of women education both at Centre and State level. Many constitutional provisions have been made and several programmes have been undertaken during various five year plans. But nevertheless their literacy rate is lagging behind the male population both at national and regional level respectively. So improvement in education is essential for them.

Realising the importance of education for nearly half of members of the society, many social scientists and thinkers drawn from different faculties have presented their research studies and well considered judicious view in rare styles on various emerging issues after the implementation of policies and programmes pertaining to women education and prescribed their well conceived thinkings for the educational development of the society in general and women folk in particular.

Based on both primary and secondary sources of data this work portrays the extent of development of women education in National as well as Regional level, the inequality in the education level of both male and female population as well as rural and urban females and their possible causes, the emerging issues which stand on the way of the development of women education, the various government policies undertaken for the development of women education, their suitability and future prospects of women education.

It is hoped that these views would stimulate the thinking of researchers, social activists, politicians and induce the planners and the administrators to look at the problems in right prospective and introduce policy measures for wholesome growth of the society benefiting the people at large.

EDITORS

ACKNOWLEDGEMENT

The Editors of this volume owe their deepest sense of gratitude and indebtedness to University Grants Commission (Eastern Regional Office) LB-8, Sector-III, Salt Lake, Kolkata-700098, for the financial support to organise a National Level Conference, otherwise it would have been impossible.

They will fail in their duty if they do not acknowledge their indebtedness to Srijukta Kalpataru Das, Honourable M.L.A., Dharmasala, Jajpur, Orissa and President Governing Body of the college, who despite of his busy schedule has come to inaugurate the U.G.C. Sponsored National Level Conference on 26th November, 2006 in the college premises 90 kms away from the state capital and addressed the delegates on the present position of Women Education, various problems faced by the women, society and the Government in developing Women Education and the possible steps which are being taken by the Government for their educational development.

Dr. Pravat Kumar Sahoo, Director, Distance Education Institute, and Professor of Education, University of Allahabad, Uttar Pradesh needs a special mention as he has delivered an elaborate presentation on "Empowerment of Women with special reference to Girl Child" in his address in the inaugural session as the Guest of Honour.

No words are adequate to express their thankfulness to Dr. Mohit Mohan Mohanty, former Director, State Institute of Education, Management Administration and Technology, Orissa Bhubaneswar for his valuable deliberation on "Women Empowerment Education and Development" as the key note speaker.

They record their sincere gratitude and extend heartful thanks to Dr. Gopal Charan Biswal, Department of Education, Radhanath Institute of Advanced Studies' in Education, Cuttack and Dr. Surekha Sundari Swain, Programme Co-ordinator, N.S.S., Utkal University, Vani Vihar, Bhubaneswar as they have successfully conducted the technical sessions of the Conference.

They are extremely thankful to Dr. V.K. Sunwani, Vice-Principal, Dr. Bhujendranath Panda, Reader both from Regional Institute of Education, Bhubaneswar, Benudhar Chinara, Reader, Department of Education, Viswa Bharati University, Shantiniketan, West Bengal and Dr. Bhabagrahi Biswal, Principal Sukinda College, Sukinda, Jajpur, who have joined the Conference as Guests of Honour and resource persons addressed the delegates on various practical problems for the low development of Women Education in different areas among different social groups and prescribed valuable suggestions for their develoment who belong to half of the society.

It would be a remiss for the Editors and the organisers of Conference if they fail to appreciate the valuable suggestions rendered by Dr. Krushna Chandra Bastia, President, All Orissa Education Society and former Principal, B.B. Mahavidyalaya, Chandikhole, Jajpur, Prof. Ramakanta Jena, former Head of the Department of Education, S.V.M. Autonomous college, Jagatsinghpur, Prof. Benudhar Saran, Former Principal, U.N.S. Mahavidyalaya, Khairabad, Mugpal, Jajpur and Dr. Yudhistir Khatua, Secretary, All Orissa Education Society during the organisation of the Conference.

The Editors are deeply indebted to the invited guests, delegates, paper writers, media persons, local elites and educated women present who despite of their own personal inconveniences came forward with all enthusiasm and sponsored quite a lot of their personal time to make the conference a grand success, otherwise the volume could have been impossible.

They are grateful to the staff and students of U.N.S. Mahavidyalaya, Khairabad, Mugpal, Jajpur (Orissa), without their co-operation organisation of Conference and publication of Conference volume could not have been imagined.

It is a great pleasure to acknowledge the inestimable help received from Prof. Rabindranath Samal, Administrative Bursar, Prof. Rama Chandra Sahoo, Sr. Lecturer in History, Dr. Susmita Mishra, Lecturer in History, Dr. Dhruba Charan Nayak, Lecturer in Oriya, Dr. Sudhansu Sekhar Mishra, Prof. in charge of U.G.C., Prof. Nrusingha Charan Tripathy, Lecturer in History, Prof. Ramesh Chandra Bhoi, Lecturer in Education, Miss Muktilata Das, Lecturer in Sanskrit, Prof. Dillip Kumar Chakra, Lecturer in English of U.N.S. Mahavidyalaya in providing unstinct co-operation and ungruding help.

To name a few they must thank Sri Surendra Kumar Tripathy, Head Clerk, Janardan Sahoo, Accountant, Rajkishore Kar, Sr. Clerk,

Biswanath Panda, Cashier, Baban Charan Dash, Accounts Clerk, Shantilata Sahu, Demonstrator Physics, Manoj Kumar Mohapatra, Demonstrator Zoology, Rabindra Kumar Khuntia, Ananta Charan Panda, Narayan Mallick, Basanta Kumar Mishra, Ananda Chandra Mishra, Narottam Maharana and Kulamani Malik, Employees of their institute for their untiring help and the people of Rasulpur Block (Orissa) for their silent support and co-operation.

M/s. Satyajeet Printers, Jachuck Lane, Buxi Bazar, Cuttack-753001 deserves special mension as he has neatly computerised the entire work.

At last they extend their thanks to M/s. Mittal Publications, New Delhi (India) for releasing this work within the record time.

EDITORS

LIST OF TABLES AND FIGURES

Tables

Figures

CONTRIBUTORS

Mohit Mohan Mohanty, Former Director, State Institute of Education, Mangement, Administration and Technogy, Orissa, Bhubaneswar.

Pravat Kumar Sahoo, Director, Distance Education Institute, Professor, Department of Education, University of Allahabad, (U.P.).

Hariballav Dash, Lecturer in Education, U.N.S. Mahavidyalaya, Khairabad, Mugpal, Jajpur-755009 (Orissa).

Puspalata Behera, Reader in Education, Govt. Women's College, Keonjhar (Orissa).

G.C. Biswal, Department of Education, Radhanath I.A.S.E., Cuttack-753 002 (Orissa).

Rajan Ku. Sahoo, Lecturer in Economics, U.N.S. Mahavidyalaya, Khairabad, Mugpal, Jajpur, Orissa-755003.

Kalpalata Patri, Lecturer (Senior Scale) in Education, Ravenshaw (Auto) College, Cuttack.

Tilottama Senapati, Lecturer in Education, Radhanath I.A.S.E., Cuttack-753 002 (Orissa).

Tarulata Devi, Lecturer in Education, P.P. College, Nischintakoili, Cuttack.

Surekha Sundari Swain, Programme Co-ordinator, N.S.S., Utkal University, Vani Vihar, Bhubaneswar, Orissa.

Sanjay Ketan Swain, Lecturer in Education, Salipur College, Salipur, Cuttack (Orissa).

Bimal Charan Swain, Lecturer in Education, N.K.C. College of Teacher Education, Angul (Orissa).

Rabinarayan Sahoo, Lecturer in Education, Nimapara College, Nimapara, Puri, (Orissa).

Rajalakshmi Das, Lecturer in Education, N. K. C. College of Teacher Education, Angul (Orissa).

Pravakar Mallick, Lecturer in Education, Tulasi Women's College, Kendrapara (Orissa).

Jayanti Satrusallya, Lecturer in Education, N.K.C. College of Teacher Education, Angul (Orissa).

Arati Satpathy, Lecturer in Education, Dharmasala Mahavidyalaya, Dharmasala, Jajpur (Orissa).

Niladri Pradhan, Research Scholar U.G.C. (NET) Regional Institute of Education (NCERT), Bhubaneswar-754022, E-mail : Pradhanniladri@yahoo.com.

Srikant Kumar Paikray, Lecturer in Education, Radhanath I.A.S.E., Cuttack.

Brundaban Patra, Lecturer in Education, Rastriya Sanskrit Sansthan (D.U.) Shree Sadashiva Campus, Puri (Orissa) 752 001.

Anil Kumar Naik, Lecturer, Department of Education, Simulia College, Markona, Balasore (Orissa) 756 126.

Sidharth Shankar Rath, Lecturer in History, U.N.S. Mahavidyalaya, Khairabad, Mugpal, Jajpur-755009 (Orissa).

Padmalaya Panda, Lecturer in Education, Gopalpur College, Gopalpur, Balasore.

K.P. Nayak, Department of Education, B.B. Mahavidyalaya, Chandikhole, Jajpur (Orissa).

Dillip Kumar Nayak, Department of Education, B.B. Mahavidyalaya, Chandikhole, Jajpur (Orissa).

Maheswar Panda, Lecturer in Education, K.S.U.B., CTE, Bhanjanagar, Ganjam, Orissa-761126.

Sadananda Mishra, Lecturer in Education, Mahima Mahavidyalaya, Joranda, Dhenkanal, Orissa.

Narendra Kumar Rana, Lecturer in Education, K.S.U.B. College of Teacher Education, Bhanjanagar, Ganjam (Orissa)-761126.

Arun Kumar Lenka, Lecturer in Education, Agarpara College, Agarpara, Bhadrak (Orissa).

Avarani Nanda, Lecturer in Education, Indira Gandhi Women's College, Cuttack, Orissa.

Yudhistir Khatua, Department of Education, J.N. College, Kuanpal, Cuttack (Orissa).

Jyostna Sahoo, Lecturer in Education, Radhanath I.A.S.E., Cuttack, Orissa.

Debi Prasanna Barik, Lecturer in Education, Choudwar College, Choudwar, Cuttack, Orissa-754071.

Akadasi Senapati, Senior Lecturer in Education, P.P. College, Nischintakoili, Cuttack (Orissa).

Leena Roy, Lecturer in Education, Dharmasala Mahavidyalaya, Jajpur (Orissa)

Namita Dash, Lecturer in Education, Bhuban Women's College, Bhuban, Dhenkanal (Orissa).

Dharanidhar Sahoo, Lecturer in Education, Kendrapara (Autonomous) College, Kendrapara.

Bijaylaxmi Das, Lecturer in Education, Sri Jaydev College of Education and Technology, Naharkanta, Khurda.

CONTENTS

1

WOMEN EMPOWERMENT, EDUCATION AND DEVELOPMENT

—Mohit Mohan Mohanty

An empowered person is characterized by (a) knowledge and competence, (b) ability to take rational decision and control, and (c) a strong self-esteem. In all the three counts women, across the globe have been overpowered by men because of historical reasons. Women's powerlessness stems from their lack of access to and control over resources — material, human, and intangible. This unequal gender relation manifests itself in different ways. Women's work and their contribution to the economy are either undervalued or outright dismissed. Their skill, knowledge, and abilities are also undervalued. They are portrayed as being weak and thereby "dependent" on men.

Some of the factors that have perpetuated such unequal power relations over ages are:

- Women's mobility has been restricted; as a result their knowledge base is also limited.
- Lack of access to education.
- Lack of access to information.

In a social milieu where women are not valued as human beings and are denied of the opportunities basic to survive as useful individuals perceive themselves as victims. To escape these vicious trappings and to enable them to acquire their rightful status in the family and society, education can act as a very powerful means. It is universally acknowledged that in societies where women are valued as men, they seem to have greater access to education. On the other hand, it has been seen that when women are educated, there is significant improvement in their status within the family and in society.

Indicators of Women's Status

- *Sex Ratio* : This is perhaps the most sensitive index of women's status. It is determined by a wide range of factors linked to public and private resources. Sex ratio is an outcome indicator that is a result of higher mortality of girl children in the 0-5 age group, neglect and discrimination in food, health care, and physical well-being at all stages of life.

  Sex ratio (calculated as number of females per 1000 males) of 1000 or more indicates a healthy status of women. In India as well as in Orissa, this ratio has demonstrated a decreasing trend from the 1901 census to the recent period.
- *Women, Work, and their Access to and Control Over Productive Assets and Resources* : It is said that women do three-fifths of the world's work, earn one-tenth of the world's income, and own one-hundredth of the world's assets. Women work, but their work is not captured in statistics. As per the Census (1991) figures, only 27 per cent women in rural areas and 9 per cent in urban areas are formally in the work force. But across the states, this figure ranged from 4 % in Punjab to 47% in Maharashtra.
- *Women's Access to Public Resources* : Public resources range from access to village commons, forest produce, water, and fuel at one end to education, training, and health care at the other end of the spectrum. Women's inability to access these resources has a profound impact on their status.
- *Control over Labour and Access to Income* : Women's level of income has direct positive impact on the improvement in the health, nutrition, and education status of their children. This does not hold true in case of men's income. Therefore, women's control over their own labour and the income earned by them is a sensitive index of women's status.
- *Women's Control over their Bodies* : One of the most glaring dimensions of gender inequality is women's lack

of control over their own bodies. Indicators like, recorded numbers of domestic and sexual violence, prevalence of abortion and resultant mortality and morbidity maternal and infant mortality rates, fertility rate, percentage of male and female sterilizations, contraceptive prevalence rates are used to assess the women's status in the family and society.

- *Access to Intangible Resources* : The relative strength or status of two groups (like men and women) is compared usually using the terms like, self-confidence, self-esteem, knowledge acquired in the experience of life, and general family environment. These are often dismissed as being intangibles. But the programmes like Women Development Programme of Rajasthan (1984) and later on its extension in the form of Mahila Samakhya have proved that such intangibles have to be addressed if we are serious about improving the status of women.
- *Law and Mechanisms for Legal Redressal* : Progressive laws and a women-friendly judiciary theoretically provide women with the opportunity to seek redressal and emphatically assert their status. Women's access to legal aid and shelters, percentage of registered cases of crimes against women that have led to conviction, outcomes of Jati Mahasabhas etc. are some indicators of legal redressal mechanisms available to women.
- *Women's Access to Decision Making Fora and Political Space* : Participation in the administrative and political bodies ensures equal say in the matters of decision making and as a direct consequence women occupy positions of power and respectability. This needs no further elaboration.
- *Female Literacy Rate* : Gender disparity becomes immediately perceivable looking at the female literacy rates vis-à-vis male literacy rates . In every state of India and in every locality the female literacy rate lags behind the male literacy rates in all the census figures. The gender differentials in literacy in India ranges from 6 (in Kerala) to 34 (in Rajasthan) as against the all India figure of 22. Female literacy rates are universally used as the indicator of women's status.

Role of Education in Empowerment

Although education is not the only means of empowering people, its role is crucial in all the means employed to raise the status of women. Dreaze and Sen (1995) point to the five distinct ways how education (and health) can be seen to be valuable to the freedom of a person (consequently for empowerment).

- Intrinsic importance,
- Instrumental personal roles,
- Instrumental social roles,
- Instrumental process roles, and
- Empowerment and distributive roles.

The influences need not work for the person who receives education. There are also interpersonal effects. One persons educational ability can be of use to another. Expansion of health and education can have influences that go much beyond the immediate personal effects.

Women's Education and Development

There is a very strong instrumental case for achieving gender equality in education. A large body of evidence shows that it is in the private and social interests of people and communities to reduce gender inequalities in education wherever they exist.

- Economic analysis has consistently shown that the private rates of return to education are significant. In most countries women experience discrimination in the labour market in terms of their earnings. However, the proportionate increase in wages (and thus rates of return) associated with an additional year of schooling at each level tend to be about same for both sexes. Where returns do differ, they more often favour women than men.
- Increasing female education has been shown to have a greater effect on overall labour supply by increasing the amount of time that women work.. By contrast, the quantity of work men wish to do seems not to be influenced by their own educational level. Accordingly, strategies to increase women's education relative to that of men will tend to increase overall labour force participation.
- A very important consequence of society investing more on education of girls and women is the changes brought about in household behaviour and practice which are

strongly associated with the increased levels of education of the mother than of the father.

- The schooling of parents (in particular of mother) increases the probability of their children — of both sexes — attending school.
- A further welcome benefit of the schooling of women concerns its well-documented negative impact on rates of fertility. Contrary to it, additional schooling of men are associated with increased fertility

All these and more direct and indirect benefits indicate that, where females have less access to schooling than males, society looses.

Gender Equality and Empowerment

The formal approach to parity is inadequate; education must adopt the substantive or corrective approach to gender equality.

- Education should not be simply concerned with equality in treatment, but equality in terms of outcomes.
- A substantive definition of equality takes into account and focuses on diversity, difference, disadvantage and discrimination.
- This approach actively questions the ways in which gendering results in the subordination of girls and women, and imposes pressures of "masculinity" on boys and men; it develops in the learner the ability to question relations of power that are central to the hierarchies of gender.
- This approach recognizes the gendered difference between girls and boys, but does not accept this difference as a given; instead, it examines the assumptions behind it, tries to assess the disadvantage resulting from it, and develops a "different" treatment that dismantles that disadvantage.
- Girls and women are also circumscribed by a gendered socialization that differs across the caste, tribe and community, and the rural-urban divide: these results in the creation of differentiated aspirations, capacities and levels of confidence. This approach to equality addresses such differences in ways that helps learners to overcome disadvantages, value their differentiated capabilities, and develop them to the fullest.

This means that process of education have to be designed to ensure that girls and women as well as their counterparts i.e., boys and men, enjoy and relate to teaching methods, curricula and experiences that empower them from diverse backgrounds to overcome disadvantages rather than reinforce their subordination. Education, in this sense, is not training but empowerment.

Empowerment Through Education Implies

(i) promoting self-recognition, a positive self-image and self-actualization,

(ii) stimulating critical thinking,

(iii) deepening understanding of the gendered structures of power, including gender,

(iv) enabling access to resources, specially to an expanding framework of information and knowledge,

(v) developing the ability to analyze the options available, and to facilitate the possibility of making informed choices, and

(vi) reinforcing the agency of women to challenge gendered structures of power and take control of their lives.

Education for Women Empowerment

The National Focus Group on Gender Issues in Education for the development of the National Curricular Framework, 2005 have made several recommendations some of which are :

- Access to education for all girls,
- Ensuring retention and quality of girls' education,
- Establish gender as a critical marker of transformation and an organizing principle,
- Establish that gender is not an women's issue — it is a people's issue,
- Critical and proactive approach to equality and empowerment of girls and women,
- Open human minds to the capacity for rational critique and enable them to envision new possibilities,
- Introduce participatory and dialogical pedagogic mode,
- Incorporate conflict as a pedagogic strategy,
- Assessment affirming a spirit of critical inquiry, and
- Curricular practices to be shaped by the life worlds of learners.

There are several paths to remove iniquitous discriminatory practices and ensuring women empowerment of which education is considered as a powerful one. The right-based arguments for removing gender inequalities, particularly in education, are of overriding importance (UNESCO, 2003). For arguments that equality cannot be afforded, or that it would generate pressures that conflict with other more pressing development priorities, are largely false. On the contrary, a committed shift towards the creation of gender equality in education can deliver a wide range of associated benefits for economic growth and for other objectives of development policy.

REFERENCES

Dreaze, Jean and Sen, Amartya (1995), Basic Education as a Political Issue, *Journal of Educational Planning and Administration,* 9(1), 1-26.

Dreaze, Jean and Sen, Amartya (1997), *India: Economic Development and Social Opportunity,* New Dethi: Oxford University Press.

Dreaze, Jean and Sen, Amartya (2003), *India: Participation and Development.* New Delhi: Oxford University Press.

King, Elizabeth M. & Anne Hill, M. (1993), *Women's Education in Developing Countries: Barriers, Benefits and Policies,* London: The John Hopkins University Press & the World Bank.

NCERT (2005), Gender Issues in Education. *In The National Curricular Framework Review 2005, National Focus Groups Position Papers (VoL III) National Concerns,* New Delhi: NCERT.

Sen, Amartya (1992), *Inequality Reexamined,* New Delhi: Oxford University Press.

UNESCO (2003). *Gender and Education for All. The Leap to Equality,* (EFA Global monitoring Report), Paris : UNESCO.

2

EMPOWERMENT OF WOMEN WITH SPECIAL REFERENCE TO GIRL CHILD

—Pravat Kumar Sahoo

Appreciating education as the basic agent of improvement in quality of life especially in the status of women came to the light by a host of studies in the second half of the preceding century. These studies highlighted the facts that women education is the key to demographic transition from high to low levels of fertility and mortality; improving health and nutrition, overcoming disadvantages they face in a men dominated society, enhancing economic productivity and contributing in meaningful way for gender equality; overcoming powerlessness and availing social equality and opportunity. These features are essentially the determinants of leading an egalitarian society that we dream for our forthcoming generation.

World Scenario

The major international conventions (Jomtien Declaration, 1990, World Education Forum, Dakar, 2000, Millenium Development Goals 2000, Biwako Millennium Frame Work, 2003) during last decades have come up with commitment of eliminating all forms of discrimination against women and girls child. As reported by the United Nations: Women are over half of the world's population, yet they do two-third of the world's work and one-tenth of the world's income and own less than one-hundredth of the world's property. The women and girlchild are the worst sufferers of educational backwardness. About 115 million children are out of school in the world of which 65 million children are girls. Two-third of the world's 875 million illiterate adults are women. A UNO report reveals :

- About 1.3 billion people are in poverty of which 70 per cent are women.
- Women earn three-fourth of the income that men earn in non-agricultural sector.
- Women occupy only 10 per cent of the parliamentary seats and only 6 per cent of cabinet positions in 55 countries around the world.
- Of the total burden of work, women carry an average of 53 per cent in developing countries and 51 per cent in industrial countries.
- Of the world's 900 million non-literate persons, 65 per cent are women due to lack of educational opportunities.
- Worldwide 76 million more boys are enrolled in primary and secondary school than girls.
- Out of world's 25 million child labour about 65 per cent is girls child. Of which 50% is in India.

In view of existing status of women and girls, former secretary general of UNO Kofi Annan (Dakar, Senegal, 26th April, 2001) has rightly remarked "there can be no lasting reduction in global poverty until girls receive the basic quality education they deserve and take their rightful place as equal partners in development". Girls' education is among the priorities of UNICEF's medium term strategic plan for 2002-05. UNICEF estimate shows that 91 developing countries and 34 industrialized countries are on course to reach the gender parity (MDG-1) at primary level of education with as many girls in school as boys. Eliminating gender disparity is clearly a steppingstone towards the achievement of primary education (MDG-2) by 2015. Gender parity is also a platform for gender equality and the empowerment of women (MDG-3), which are essential for achievement of other MDGs such as reducing child mortality improving maternal health and alleviating poverty.

The concept of 'empowerment of women' dates back to the International Women's Conference at Nairobi in 1985. The conference defined women's empowerment as redistribution of social power and control of resources in favour of women. The growing concern for bringing an attitudinal change in society for empowerment of women and girls child got culminated in the declaration of 2001 as the 'Empowerment Year for Women'. The very concept of women empowerment includes realization of gender parity and a continuous process of enhancing skills, capacity building, gaining self-confidence and meaningful participation in decision-making activities.

Challenges and Initiatives at Local Level

The women constitute nearly half of India's population. But in each and every walk of life they are lagging behind the progress of male population. The female literacy is very low i.e. 54.16% in comparison to the male literacy of 75.8% (Census, 2001). Female oppression caused by family, community and religion is one of the root reasons of low literacy among females (Saroja, 1994), Discrimination and gender bias were found in relation to nutrition, nourishment, child rearing practices and education of female children in comparison to male children (Jha, 2002). It is the ground reality in the Indian context that men have dominated each and every field of knowledge and work. To meet the existing challenges of equity of men and women the National Policy for Empowerment of Women, 2001 envisages introduction of a gender perspective in the budgeting process as an operational strategy. In this context, the Ninth Plan document (1997-02) incorporated women component plan (WCP) directing both the central and state governments to ensure that not less than 30 per cent of the funds/benefits are earmarked for women related sectors. The Tenth Plan document (2002-07) reinforces commitment to gender budgeting to establish gender differential impact and to translate gender commitments into budgetary commitments. The Tenth Plan proposes that both Women Component Plan and Gender Budgeting should play a complementary role and ensure through both preventive and post facto action, that women receive their rightful share from all women related general development sectors.

The UNDP Report (1997) reveals that Indian women get only 25% of the share in the earned income. Work burden on them is extreme as they work 69 hours a week while men work 59 hours. The Report observes that Indian women suffer on two sides (i) because of an impoverished society, (ii) because they are women. The heinous factors like gender bias, age old prejudice, blind discrimination against female children, prioritizing male children have led to female feticides and female infanticide. To give an instance more than four million female children joined the rank of India's "missing women" and 1.2 million lives were snuffed out either abortion or post natal murder according to an estimation made during the decade 1981-91. (Rajasthan, Haryana) No doubt, the violence against women is an ever-existing phenomenon in almost all the societies either in overt or covert form. Concerted efforts by the researchers, women organizations, academics, social workers and journalists have brought to lime light the women issues like wife abuse, dowry victimization, divorce, raping, burning and killing of women, community oppression on women, opposing schooling of female children, low female literacy in rural and tribal areas as the burning social problems during last three decades. (Supreme Court Judgement Bill in the Parliament.)

Progressive thinkers across the ideological spectrum agree that education is one of the most significant factors to bring a paradigm shift in the status of women. The skewed sex ratio and the high infant mortality are a such a cause as an effect of the gender disparity in educational opportunity. It is recognized that in rural India, out of every 100 girls enrolled in class-I only six entered class XII. In urban areas, the situation is also similarly alarming where only fourteen girls of every 100 make it to class XII. In rural area a majority of girls drop out at primary level. Out of the 100 who enroll in class-I only 40-join class-V. The drop out rate is much higher among the disadvantaged groups, the scheduled castes and the scheduled tribes. The linguistic and religious minorities and families living in inaccessible forests and hill locked areas are also major sufferers of schooling system. If they will be deprived of seeing the light of a knowledge society the human rights for women may be experienced in remote possibility. It is high time to ponder on the issue of fundamental rights of children especially of girls child in getting free and compulsory education in their formative years of schooling (6-14 years).

Girls' Specific Interventions

Gender disparity has been considered as a serious issue in our national planning and development strategies. Several constitutional provisions have in-built philosophy in promoting empowerment of women and girls child. Prohibition of discrimination on the grounds of religion, race, caste and sex (Art. 15), equal opportunity in public employment (Art. 16) and making education as fundamental right of children (Art. 21 by virtue of 93rd Amendment Act, 2002) to ensure that all children are in schools, are some of the constitutional landmarks to defend the rights of the women and girls child.

The National Policy on Education, 1986, states that "Education will be used as an agent of basic change in the status of women.

Table 2.1 : Interventions and Their Coverage at Elementary Level

Interventions	*Main Features*	*Issues to be addressed*	*Coverage*
Mahila Samakhya (MS) (1989)	Promoting women's education and empowerment of women in rural areas, particularly women in socially and economically mariginalized groups.	Child marriage, child labour, violence against women	9,000 villages in 53 districts, 10 states
Girls Specific DPEP Intervention	Targeting low female literacy districts, tribal and other disadvantaged communities	High Dropouts, Gender disparity, qualitative teaching learning activities at primary stage	236 districts of 15 states (Phase-I and II)
Kasturba Gandhi Swatantrata Vidyalaya (KGSV) (2002)	Ensuring access and quality education to girls in the form of residential schools	Access and quality issues of girls education in hard-to-reach areas, tribal communities and minorities having low female literacy	Wide coverage of selected hard-to-reach areas with 750 residential schools for girls in the country
National Programme for Education of Girls at Elementary Level (NPEGEL) (2003)	Promoting education of girls at the elementary stage especially from disadvantaged communities. The programme is implemented in the forms of additional components under SSA.	Areas with high gender disparity, educationally backward blocks, having below 10 per cent female literacy among the disadvantages communities: SC/ST/minorities.	2,656 educationally backward blocks in 21 states of the country.

(CARE India's Girls' Education Project in Rajasthan & U.P.)

The national education system will play a positive, interventionist role in the empowerment of new values through re-designed curricula, text books, training and orientation of teachers decision-makers and administrators and the active involvement of educational institutions."

The NPE, 1986 triggered off a number of girls specific interventions during the preceding couple of decades especially in the field of elementary education. Major interventions are given in the Table 2.1:

School Participation of Girls Child

The UNESCO Global Monitoring Report, 2005 ascertains that India is one of the 40-odd countries not likely to meet most of the Education For All goals even by 2015. The Sarva Shiksha Abhiyan (SSA) has kept a tougher target of achieving the completion of five years of primary schooling of all children by 2007 and the completion of eight years of elementary schooling by 2010. Likewise, the SSA targets at bridging the gender gaps at primary stage by 2007 and at elementary stage by 2010. While the official figures of enrolment at primary stage claims to be 93 per cent, the recent sample survey conducted by a voluntary organization Pratham shows only 73 per cent of enrolled children attend the school. With reference to this estimate a staggering 60 million children (out of 210 million children in the age group of 6-14 years) are not in school. It has also been reported that about 50 per cent children dropouts without completing the cycle of elementary education (Govinda, 2006). It is estimated that about 70 per cent of them are girls. The proportion of out of school girls are higher in rural and tribal areas (Sahoo and Das. 2006).

Girls Participation in Tribal Schools

A study carried out by Das (2006) in the tribal belt of Orissa ascertains the following status about the school participation of girls (Table 2.2).

It can be observed that out of total girls child in the age group of 6-14 years in the sample villages about 75 per cent are enrolled in the school. The study further shows that only about 56 per cent of enrolled children attend the school. This would bring the figure of out of school children to 44 per cent of the total children.

The most alarming situation is the retention rate of tribal girls at primary stage that is only 7.4 per cent. If one takes this into account the number of out of school children rises enormously.

Table 2.2 : Context wise School Participation of Tribal Girls

(in per cent)

Indicators	*Village Development*		*Nature of School*			*Access to School*		*Total*
	UDV	*MDV*	*OPS*	*RS*	*NPS*	*EAS*	*PAS*	
Enrolment	70.02	79.2	84.42	70.65	72.77	78.08	71.14	74.61
Attendance	48.17	63.33	50.72	74.99	41.54	63.00	48.50	55.75
Retention	4.44	10.37	6.25	8.18	7.79	5.57	9.24	7.40
Sample Schools (N)	9	9	6	6	6	9	9	1.8

Note: UDV—Under Developed Village. MDV—Moderately Developed Village. OPS—Old Primary School. RS—Residential Sevashram Primary School. NPS—New Primary School. EAS—Easily Accessible School, PAS—Poorly Accessible School.

Source: Das, 2006 ongoing doctoral study, Dept. of Education, A.U.

The other findings of the study gain significance in the contexts of village development, nature of school and access to school.

- The village development counts positively in relation to enrolment, attendance .and retention of girls child in tribal villages. It is observed that girls' enrolment and attendance in moderately developed villages are higher to the corresponding proportions in under developed villages. With regard to retention there exists substantial difference between underdeveloped and moderately developed villages. In other words it can be said that moderately developed villages are able to retain the girls child better at primary stage of education as compared to underdeveloped villages.
- The nature of school breakup ascertains that the enrolment figures are higher in old primary school, which has been followed by new primary and residential sevashram primary school. However, with reference to attendance and retention residential sevashram primary school is witnessed in better status in comparison to old and new primary schools. The old primary is observed with better girls' attendance than new primary. But, the girls child are better retained in new primary than old primary. It can be said that the school participation of girls child are better nurtured in a residential nature of school.
- Access to school divide ascertains enrolment and attendance of girls child in favour of easily accessible

school. So far as retention is concerned poorly accessible school performs better in retaining the girls child in comparison to easily accessible schools. Further, it is observed that out of school children are in high number in case of poorly accessible schools, which suffers a lot due to teacher absenteeism, lack of awareness and engagement of children in sibling care and household activities. The girls child of easily accessible villages quickly part away from the school and engage themselves in production and earning activities. It would be worth mentioning that the figure of girls child labour are higher in easily accessible villages in comparison to poorly accessible villages, which causes a stunning reversal in their retention.

Target Free Women's Participation

The Government of India in 1996, declared the entire country 'target free' while withdrawing family planning targets in selected districts (Ramachandran, 2000). The main focus is still on women but with one significant difference i.e. is concentrating on the holistic participation of women in enhancing the quality of life in the context of a developing society, which is nonetheless diseased with a volley of threats to women's rights.

Education is key to quality of life. Supporting women and girls child in realizing their potential and ensuring their sharings in sustainable development; involving them in the process of decision-making and policy development and enabling them to participate in production, employment and income generating activities as well as enhancing their participation in education, family and health care, art, literature, music, politics, science and technology, sports, culture, environment and population related policies and development will certainly empower them to contribute at par with men.

Conclusion and Implications

Education system must play a significant role in promoting values of an egalitarian society. 'I'he Indian Society that suffers from various stigmas with regard to equal status of women in different spheres of life must be transformed into a modern and humane society. Making school curriculum more dynamic and vibrant towards women's participation and their role in social development processes must accelerate the efforts made so far in this direction.

In this context the school curriculum must perceive the contextual significance of gender equity and rights of women cutting across the boundaries of subject areas and disciplines.

The paper has many seminal implications for the policy makers, curriculum designers, textbook writers, heads of the institutions, researchers, journalists, social thinkers and reformers, women organizations and various intervening government and non-government organizations.

- The policy makers should do policy-mapping exercises and develop strategies in relation to empowerment of women and girls child.
- The curriculum designers and text books writers should incorporate with equal weightage to feminine events and patterns keeping in mind the rights of the girls child and women of an egalitarian society.
- The heads of the institutions should take care of providing every kind of scope and opportunities for the betterment of female students.
- The researchers should keep on interest in exploring the threats to the rights and living of girls child and women in present contexts.
- The journalists and writers should take interest in preparing and publishing the news items/articles/papers related to various issues of girls and women with a view to bring awareness to the society.
- The social thinkers and reformers should initiate women's movement against existing social stigmas and organize awareness activities encouraging direct participation of women in various development activities.
- The women organizations should express their concerns over women issues and initiate women involvement in resolving their common problems.
- The intervening government and non-government organizations should invite the participation of women in identifying and preserving their rights on global standard. They should integrate income generating activities with awareness programme in enhancing quality of life.

REFERENCES

Census Report, 2001, Govt. of India.

Das, B.C. (2006), *A Study of DPEP Intervention in Tribal Education and Its Effectiveness in Orissa*, Department of Education, University of Allahabad.

Govinda, R. (2006), Class Struggle, *India Today,* Vol. XXXI (15).

Govt. of India (2002), *Selected Educational Statistics,* New Delhi: MHRD.

Govt. of India (1986), *National Policy on Education, 1986,* New Delhi: MHRD.

http:/www.unicef.org/infobycountry/india25 853 .html

Jha, P.K. (2002), *Educating Human Rights,* Agra: Bhargava.

Levin, L. (1998), *Human Rights,* UNESCO.

NIEPA (2002). *National Consultation on Framing the Follow up Legislation to the Fundamental Right to Education,* 14-15th June, New Delhi: NIEPA.

Ramachandran, Vimala (2000), *Education and the Status of Women, Education For All-Year 2000 Assessment,* New Delhi: MHRD/NIEPA.

Sahoo, P.K. and Das, B.C. (2006), *Primary Education in the Tribal Belt of Orissa,* In Rath, G.C. (ed.) Tribal Development in India, New Delhi/ Thousand Oaks/London: SAGE.

Saroja, N. (1994), *Gender Issues in Education,* Progressive Educational Herald 8(4).

UNICEF (1997), *UNDP Report, 1997.*

UNICEF (2005), *Millennium Development Goals (MDG),* cited in Progress for Children, A Report card on Gender Parity and Primary Education No. 2, April.

WOMEN EDUCATION —Emerging Issues and Rethinking

—HARIBALLAV DASH

Introduction

Women constitute an important segment of society and perform multiple roles as mothers, housewives and wage earners. They are the agents of change. Education is essential to enable them to participate and benefit from the development process. It can help them to enhance their literacy skills, better hygiene caring for family health, utilization of their leisure time to develop the vocational skills for their economic enhancement to fight against exploitation and to conquer the disadventage and discrimination which they suffer from. Their dependence disappears, awareness increases leading to over all development and helping the nation to prosper. Napolean has rightly said "Give me an educated mother I shall promise you the birth of a civilized Nation".

Need of Women Education

There is a positive co-relation between women literacy rate and life expectancy, while illiteracy is invariably associated with poverty, malnutrition, deprivation, high mortality high population growths and all other aspects of under development, women education becomes imperative.

The sex ratio, which was 972 per 1000 males in 1901, has declined to 927 in 1991. The adverse sex ratio for females and its decline was attributed mainly to higher mortality among females as compared to males. Despite being first country in the world to start family planning programme using Government machinery, India still has a high fertility rate of 3.6%. Illiteracy, ignorance malnutrition, multiple pregnancy with no proper birth spacing make many of our women incapable to maintain the new born, survival. All the aforesaid problems are mainly concerned with the lack of women's education.

Lack of, education, training and low level of literacy not merely excluded women from social, economic and political power but knowledge power as well.

Women while comprising half of the humanity contribute 2/3rd of the world's work hours, earn only 1/3rd of the tiotal income and own less than 1/10th of the world resources. Women literates constitute 44.5 per cent of the total literates. The per cent of women in Government at ministrial level is 10% while the female economic activity is 42 percent of the total economic activity.

Similarly in political horizon out of 27,50,865 elected Gram panchayat members all over India only 5,77,270 are women. Out of 1,48,697 elected panchayat samiti members 37,611 are women and out of 12,516 members in Zilla Parishads 2,993 are women. Women are lacking in these fields due to lack of education.

Objectives

Considering the importance of women education in all spheres of society this study was planned with the following objectives.

- # To study the extent of development of women education in National as well as Regional level.
- # To study the inequality in the education level of both male and female population as well as rural and urban females and their possible causes.
- # To find out the emerging issues which stand on the way of the Development of women education.
- # To study the various government policies undertaken for the development of women education, their suitability and future prospects of development of women education.

Methodology

The paper was prepared collecting information from various sources. Several books, research reports both of Government and Non-Government organizations have been consulted.

Development of Women Education in both National as well as Regional Level

Since independence various Commissions and Committees have recommended for the development of women education both at centre and state level. Many constitutional provisions have been made and several programmes have been under taken during various five year plans. Due to implementation of the programmes literacy rate of females in India has increased from 8.86 per cent in 1951 to 54.16 per cent in 2001. Similarly in Orissa female literacy has increased from 4.52% in 1951 to 50.97%. But still after more than 50 years of Indian independence 46% of women in the country and 49% in Orissa are illiterate, which has serious consequences. While this rate is compared with male literacy it is more precarious. While female literacy in India is 54.16% in 2001 it is 75.85 per cent in case of males. In Orissa while rate of literacy is 50.97 per cent in case of females it is 75.95% in case of males, which has been shown in Table No. 3.1. So the females are lagging behind the males in literacy front both in India and Orissa.

The rural urban difference in literacy is more pronouced in case of women than for men. Among the rural female the literacy rate is 46.58 per cent against 72.99 per cent amont the urban female population in India. The corresponding figures for rural and urban male population on the other hand are 71.8 per cent and 86.42 per cent respectively.

Table 3.1 : Literacy Rates of India and Orissa, 1951-2001

Census Years	*India*			*Orissa*		
	Persons	*Males*	*Females*	*Persons*	*Males*	*Females*
1	2	3	4	5	6	7
1951	18.33	27.16	8.86	15.80	27.32	4.52
1961	28.30	40.40	15.35	21.66	34.68	8.65
1971	34.45	45.96	21.97	26.18	38.29	13.92
1981	43.57	56.38	29.76	33.62	46.39	20.60
1991	52.21	64.13	39.29	49.09	63.09	34.68
2001	65.38	75.85	54.16	63.61	75.95	50.97

From the analysis of figures it was concluded that women education is at a backward stage.

There are several causes for the backwardness of women education. Poverty, economic backwardness, of parents, engagement of girl child in household chores care of siblings, location of schools at distant places, lack of female teacher in schools, formal educational system and lack of good envionment of the school, low status to women in society are some of the causes of low women literacy in India.

If the following measures like financial provision to the parents of students, scholarship, uniform and text books free of cost will be provided to the students, women students are freed from household chores through opening of pre-schools, schools are opened in every village or basti, separate schools are set up for women, number of women teachers increased, communication facilities developed, non-formal system of education is developed and attitude of parents and people in community is changed some improvements may be seen in the field of women education.

Conclusion

Education the agent of basic change in the status of women demands commitment and active involvement of all concerned. So when special attention will be given by government with active participation of the people, a new era will be created in the field of women education.

REFERENCES

Dashora Rakesh & Anushree Sharma, (2003), *Role of Tribal Women in Education,* Yojana ; Publication Division, Ministry of I & B, Patiala House, New Delhi-110001, Vol 47, No. 6, June, pp. 40-43.

Jayanthi C., (2001), *Catching up Education*, Yojana, Publication Division Ministry of I & B, Patiala House, New Delhi - 110001, Vol 45, Aug, pp. 13-16.

Jena S.K., (2004), *Population Studies*, Elegant Publications, Bhubaneswar - 751 002, Orissa.

Khan Mohsin Ali, (2001), *Women Education still a Distant Dream*, Yojana, Publication Ministry of I & B, Patiala House, New Delhi - 110001, Vol 45, Dec. pp. 40-43.

Sekhar K & B.S. Vasudeva Rao, (2001), *Empowerment of Women through Distance Education,* Yojana, Publication Division, Ministry of I & B, Patiala House, New Delhi-110001, Vol 45, Dec., pp. 44-45.

Sekhar Madhu R., (2001), *Girls Education Opening the Window into the World*, Yojana, Publication Division, Ministry of I & B, Patiala House, New Delhi-110001, Vol 45, Nov., pp. 46-47.

GENDER DISPARITY IN EDUCATION—Future Prospects of Women Education

—PUSPALATA BEHERA

India to-day is striving out into the Modern world looking ahead to new science and technology, new types of employment and a new dynamism in economic growth, but not ahead in paying specal attention to the scenario of educaon of women. Women education is considered to be a vital component of the overall strategy of securing equity and social justice in education.

Education is a human endeavour which is looked upon as a means to untangle and straighten the complex web of he problems facing the modern world. One of these, which is still not perceived as a problem by almost half of the worlds' inhabitants, is the gender imbalance in the access, participation and involvement in the process of development. The beginning of the civilization must have been based on equal contribution from both men and women but somehow during the voyage of time, women were left behind. This deliberate or unintentional trailing has resulted in an immense gap between the two founders. Gender became an important clearing criteria with separate sets of values, modes of behaviour, vocations resulting in the emergence of a system unjust to women. Women were denied freedom, a positive share in social and political power and even the right to individuality. Infact, the dignity of the human being has been elusive to her, till date.

India gained independence and the Indian constitution granted equal access to women in every sphere of life which leads to the increase in educational opportunities for women. Most policy statements attempted to soft-pedal the deep rooted prejudices and thus a slow-increase in the rate of education among women is seen.

Education, has a wider meaning "Sa Vidya Ya Vimuktya" implying that it is the knowledge which liberates. The literacy campaign means to liberate women from the shackles of mass ignorance as reading and writing widens one's horizon leading to self-confidence, self-assertion and self-dependence. If we compare the progress of literacy among male and female a huge disparity is evident.

Table 4.1 : Progress of Literacy

(In per cent)

Year	*Literate of Total females*	*Literate of Total Males*	*Total*
1951	8.86	27.16	18.33
1961	15.34	40.40	28.31
1971	21.97	45.95	34.45
1981	29.75	56.50	43.67
1991	39.29	64.13	52.21
2001	54.16	75.85	65.38

There has been a continuous progress in total male and female literacy rates in the previous decades. It is evident from the above table that though male and female literacy rates have increased over the period, there is an undesirable continuance of gender disparity. There is a long and wide gap i.e. 21 .70 per cent in 2001 census between male and female literacy rates, which is serious enough to cause concern. The gap should be brought down from 21.70 per cent to 10 per cent.

In spite of having a massive system of higher education, only six percent youth of the relevant age group of 17 to 24 years is receiving higher education as compared to France (50%), U.S.A. (81%) and Canada (99.8%). At the same time the system has been failed to cater to the heterogeneity of the society. So far as the higher education of women is concerned a large difference between male and female enrolment is found. No doubt after independence, particularly in the last decade of the last millennium, higher education envisaged a tremendous quantitative expansion. The gross enrolment in higher education in 1991 was 44,25,247 lakh which has risen to 83,99,443 lakh in the year 2001. Also it was hoped that changing attitude in favour of gender equity will contribute in raising the number of women in higher education. But it was not happened.

There has been a phenomenal growth in the number of women's enrolment in higher education since independence. Women enrolment was less than 10 per cent at the time of independence and it has risen to 39.04 per cent in 2001-2002. The table - 4.2 shows the progress of higher education of women for the last seven years.

Table 4.2 : Progress of Higher Education of Women

Year	*Total Enrolment*	*Women Enrolment*	*Percentage of women*
1995-96	65,74,005	23,63,607	36%
1996-97	68,42,598	25,14,511	37%
1997-98	72,60,418	27,22,062	37%
1998-99	77,05,520	29,32,993	38%
1999-00	80,50,607	31,12,090	39%
2000-01	83,99,443	33,06,410	39.4%
2001-02	88,21,095	35,14,450	39.84%

Thus, India witnessed only 3.84 per cent growth in women's access to higher education for the last seven years. Despite the incorporation of number of progressive programmes and policies to safeguard the interest of women and to bring them to the mainstream of higher education, the progress of women in higher education is far from satisfactory.

Gender inequality tends to lower the productivity of labour and leads to increase poverty, lack of security, opportunity and empowerment which lower the quality of life for both men and women, while women and girls are treated in-equally. It directly affects the development of society hindering poverty reduction.

Major Reasons for Low Literacy

A low participation in the field of education compels us to look at the reasons for the inequity in the participation in the progress and development of the country.

- The desperate levels of socio-economic development and social stratification adversely affect the position of women.
- Poverty affects the female education.
- The objective of 'boys and girls' education differ in society. Though education of male is looked upon as an

investment for the future source of income for the family, the education of female is more an obligation and obligation first to be ignored in case of crisis.

- Social believes like early marriage, seclusion of girls etc. also have negative effects on women's education.
- Early marriage and dowry. Marriage is still considered as the main career for girls.
- The girls pursuing higher courses in science and technology, the male dominated environment, may face dangers of negative social reputation.
- Social constraints like the distance of schools, seclusion of girls, absence of female teachers, unsatisfactory transport facility, etc. come in the way of women's education.
- Non-availability of 'girls'-only institution in the vicinity also leads to dropout.
- Shortage of women teachers. Only 27.8 per cent of all teachers at school stage are women.
- Lack of home town engineering institutions.
- Besides these, unfortunately there is a built in system of gender discrimination within the schools. This is reflected in content matter of text books and also access of girls of certain kinds of courses.

Future Prospects of Women Education

The destiny of Nation is moulded and fashioned through education and it is true that, the education of women has a strategic importance. Women are the most, reliable indicator of a country's character. The most urgent priority is to ensure access to, improve the quality of education for girls and women. Education for women and girls has positive effects on family welfare. It is usually women who take the lead in matters of nutrition in making the world intelligible to the child and in socializing children in to the family and community. Improving early childhood care is dependent on the better education of women and girls.

If we want the world to be a better place to live in, we must treat women at par with men, as a bird can not fly on one wing or unequal wings. The realization though had been there but it had been on more or less on individual basis, like Swami Vivekananda said "Educate your women first and leave them to themselves, then they will tell you what reforms are necessary for them". An effort at global level is seen in the decade (1975-85) being declared as "International Decade of Women" to work for equality development and peace by the United Nations at an International Conference on women in Mexico city in 1975.

The Secretary General Mrs. H.Sipila expressed "Half of humanity that is women have yet to go a long way to achieve equality of status and opportunities along men. Equality with men and women does not exist. It is still a great disadvantage to be born female.

An educated mother learns to protect children from exposure to health risks, and thus supports sound physical and mental development. Intelligence needs early stimulation which an educated mother provides.

Though the literacy rate in rural areas increased from about 36 per cent in 1981 to 59 per cent in 2001, the corresponding rates in urban areas were about 67 and 80 per cent, respectively thus rural-urban gap has although declined from about 31 to 21 percentage but the variation is still very wide. During this period literacy rate for males increased from about 56 per cent in 1981 to nearly 76 per cent in 2001. The corresponding change in female literacy rate has been from around 30 per cent to 54 per cent. On the whole the decline in gender gap, which peaked in 1981 at 26.6 percentage and was 21.7 percentage points in 2001 is less impressive.

Education is the factor that plays the most crucial role in development of the status of women. All possible steps like the central Governments new initiative i.e. Sarva Shikshya Abhiyan the programme which aims at universalisation of education helps to the girl students to achieve their economic, social, cultural and political growth and welfare.

The empowerment of women is not a reaction to lit back at the system and reversing. The gender dis-examination but is a systematic approach to increase meaningful participation in the process of development. For this endeavour, education is the most effective tool. Education will bring women's empowerment by enhancing self-esteem, self-confidence building a positive image of women by recognizing their contribution to the society, polity and economy developing ability to think critically, speeding up decision making and actions through collective process enhancing access to legal literacy regarding rights, opportunities, encouraging economic independence and most important is ensuring equal participation in development process.

Empowering women socio-economically through increased awareness of their rights and duties as well as to resources is a decisive step towards greater security for them. It means equal status to the women, opportunity and freedom to develop themselves.

The Government of India had declared the year 2001 as the year of women's Empowerment with the following aims—

(1) To create and raise large scale awareness of women.

(2) To initiate and accelerate action to improve access to and control of resources by women.

(3) To create an environment to enhance self confidence and autonomy of women.

The National Policy on Empowerment of women suggested the following objectives for development of women education.

(i) Creating an environment through positive economic and social policies for women development and enable them to realize their full potential.

(ii) To provide opportunities to women to enjoy all human rights and freedom in political, social, economic, cultural spheres as men.

(iii) Equal access to participation and decision making of women in social, political and economic life of the Nation.

(iv) Equal access to women to health care, quality education, carrier and vocational guidance, employment, equal remuneration, occupational health and safety, social security and public office etc.

(v) Elimination of all forms of discrimination against women.

(vi) Changing societal attitude and community practices by active participation and involvement of both men and women.

(vii) Mainstreaming a gender perspective in the development process.

Remedial Measures

In order to bring women to the central-stage of development and enabling them to take a lead role in the social and economic systems the following steps may be adopted.

Compulsory Education

Education has been regarded as an effective tool for women's empowerment. Eradication of illiteracy is the first step, because when a woman is educated, the whole family is educated and the social evils, such as illiteracy of girl children, child labour, female infanticide and other superstitious practices are much less. It is education that kindles the urge for independence, hard-work, achievement and self-actualization. It inculcates human and spiritual values. Education upto a minimum of 10th standard must be made available and should be compulsory for every child. All facilities i.e. hostel facilities, residential facilities to women teachers should be provided. The village education committee and the Mahila Samiti should initiate motivation programmes to ensure regular attendance and retention of girls students in the school. Attendance scholarship, incentives for good academic performance, mid-day-meal and free uniform, easy distance of school, teaching learning process should be attractive, and at least 50 per cent of women teachers should be appointed in the school. Education for women has to be regarded as major concern of the community.

Employment

Women should find appropriate employment to support themselves, for which the EDP'S, awareness programmes, conferences, workshop etc. can help them in industrial business units.

Formation of Self-Help Groups

Women should unite themselves into social groups called self-help groups for their own progress and the progress of the community.

Credit Facilities

Liberal supply of credit along with other financial and non-financial incentives help in promoting self-employment among women. Loans must be sanctioned on the capacity and security. NGO'S, SHGS and other development agencies should initiate for the disbursement of credit as per the project needs. Training and technical consultancy services must be made available close to their station.

Mental Revolution

For the development of women education, there should be a revolutionary change in the perception and attitude of both men and women towards women. Women are in no way inferior to men and they have already imprinted their mark in all most all walks of life. Their capacity to endure and persevere is an accepted fact.

Being the better half of the total population all facilities should be provided to them as women, working shoulder to shoulder with men or independently towards development. They should cherish emotional intellectual and economic freedom. Because when women move forward, the family moves, the village moves and the nation moves. So it is the duty of all concerned to provide the women with the right environment and impetus to push them through this current stage of transition from family burden to community leader.

5

ROLE OF EDUCATION IN WOMEN'S EMPOWERMENT AND NATIONAL DEVELOPMENT —A Rethinking

—G.C. BISWAL

The most important activity of mankind is the development of man himself. Since the dawn of history, this has been and still is the task and mission of women. It is women who transmit the heritage of the past to the future generations. If the past, the present and future were not linked by her tender body into an organic whole, there would have neither any civilization nor any history. It is said 'the hand that rocks the cradle rules the world'. In the apron strings of women is hidden the revolutionary energy which can establish paradise on earth.' (Dr. Rajendra Prasad). It is a fact that women enjoyed positions of authority and eminence in the past and now some of them have been treated as objects of trade, repression and atrocities by their male counterparts.

- This above fact is highlighted in the fourth report on 'Human Development in Asia, the Gender Question'. Women do not enjoy the same basic human rights as men and are continuously discriminated in job, governance, education and healthcare.
- This region has the lowest literacy and largest gaps in literacy rates of Male and Females. Discrimination begins before birth.
- The Commonwealth Plan of Action on Gender Development (1995) focuses on a vision - A world in which men and women have equal rights and opportunities Women are respected and valued as equal partners in

establishing the values of social justice, equity, democracy, human rights, to ensure sustainable economic and social development for all nations.

- The 4th World Conference on Women Beijing (1995).
- Gender issue as a crucial component in the Deve'opment process.
- Women take their full place in the world of 21st century.
- UNESCO - Aims at a gender inclusive culture to promote sustainable development.
- The key dimensions — Empowerment, co-operation, security.

Factual Evidences of Discrimination in Men and Women

The gap between men and women in different dimensions in education are found from the following tables.

Table 5.1 : The Rate of Literacy with Gap Both at the State & National Level

Year	*Orissa*			*India*		
	M	*F*	*G*	*M*	*F*	*G*
1951	27.30	4.50	22.80	27.16	8.86	18.30
1961	34.70	8.60	26.10	40.40	15.34	25.06
1971	38.29	13.92	24.37	45.95	21.97	23.98
1981	46.90	21.11	25.79	56.37	29.75	26.62
1991	63.09	34.68	28.41	64.13	39.29	24.84
2001	75.95	50.97	24.98	75.85	54.16	21.69

The above data revealed that

- The gap is widening and approaching the condition that prevailed in 1951.
- The gap betaeen Female and Male literacy rate in Orissa is more than what is found in India except (1981).

Table 5.2 : Rural-Urban gap in Female Literacy

Class	*Rural*	*Urban*
I	100	100
V	40	82
VIII	18	62
IX	09	32
XII	01	14

Table 5.3 : Women's Enrolment to Total Enrolment in Higher Education

Sl.No.	*Year*	*Percentage of women enrolled*
1.	1995-96	36%
2.	1996-97	37%
3.	1997-98	37%
4.	1998-99	38%
5.	1999-2000	39%
6.	2000-01	39.4%
7.	2001-02	39.84%

Source: UGC Annual Report 2001-02.

Table 5.4 : Faculty wise Women's Enrolment 2001-02

Sl.No.	*Faculty*	*Percentage*
1.	Arts	51.59
2.	Science	19.90
3.	Comerce/Management	16.56
4.	Education	1.69
5.	Engg. & Tech.	3.75
6.	Medicine	3.50
7.	Agriculture	0.26
8.	Veterinary Sc.	0.09
9.	Law	1.62
10.	Others	0.84
		100

Table 5.5 : State wise Women's Enrolment to Total Enrolment 2001-02

S.No.	*State*	*Women Percentage*
1.	Andhra Pradesh	39.1
2.	Arunachal Pradesh	29.7
3.	Bihar	23.0
4.	Jharkhand	30.5
5.	Kerala	60.0
6.	Orissa	34.6
7.	Rajasthan	32.6
8.	Uttar Pradesh	35.4
9.	West Bengal	39.3

Girls account for 81 million of the 130 million out of school children. Consider as the nine high population countries collectively, female enrolment increased from 42% to 44% from 1980 to 1990. Of the 948 millions adult illiterates in the world women account for more than 60% adult illiterate.

Role of Education in Empowerment of Women

The world declaration on Education of All in 1990 stated that the most urgent priority is to ensure access to, and improve the quality of education of girls and women and to remove every obstacle that hampers their active participation. Education opens the door to opportunity and choice for women. It is the key to overcoming oppressive customs and traditions that have relegated girls and women to the status of 'second-class citizen's in their families and in their societies said. Dr. Natis Sadik, Executive director of the UNFPA. Beyond being the basic human right, the education of women is perhaps the most critical factor in reducing fertility levels and infant mortality.

Women Empowerment through Literacy and Education

Pillai (1995) quoted empowerment as an active, multidimensional process, which enables women to realize their full identity and powers in all spheres of life.

The International women's Conference defined empowerment as a redistribution of social power and control of resources in favour of women. Power has to be acquired, exercised, sustained and preserved.

Women's Economic Potentialities Improve with Education

Research indicates that each additional year a young girl stays in school translates into a 10 to 20 per cent increase in wages. Studies in india confirm that women who had completed high school earned one and half times more than those without any education, and women with technical training earned three times more than illiterate women.

Women's Education and its Linkage with Population Control

Empirical evidence exists showing the relationship between women's education and a slow down of population growth. Educating girls is three times more likely to lower family size than educating boys. Girls with eight years of education marry later; have a preference for smaller family. In Brazil, illiterate women have 6.5 children on average where as women with secondary education have 2.5 children.

Women's Education and Child Mortality Rate

Educated mothers are more likely to follow sound hygienic and nutritional practices and seek medical help when their children are ill. Literate mothers with less than six years of education have an average infant mortality rate of 100 whereas the children of illiterate mothers have mortality rate up to 170 per 1,000 live births.

Women's Education and Enrolment Figure

Educated mothers understand the value of educating their children. In India the TLC campaign have led to increase in admission figures in primary schools.

Process of Women's Empowerment

The process of women empowerment passes through five successive stages (Longwe, 1990)

(i) Welfare—Basic needs of women must be satisfied.

(ii) Access—Access to education, Land and Credit.

(iii) Conscientization—Action to fill up gender gap and discrimination.

(iv) Participation—Organizing themselves, working collectively for decision making.

(v) Control—Make decisions, play active role in development process.

Education itself is the basic requirement of woman. It is essential for empowerment. Access to Education paves the way for educating. It is education that brings Conscientization, Education helps in participation and control of resources for the world. Education forum (26-28 April, 2000) made a commitment to the attainment of the following goals.

- Ensuring that by 2015 all children (Girls) belonging to minorities have access to free and compulsory primary education of good quality.
- Achieving a 50% empowerment in Adult Literacy by 2015 for women.
- Equal access to basic and contributing Education for All.
- Eliminating adults gender disparity in primary, secondary education by 2005.
- Achieving gender equality in education by 2015.

Targets/Goals of Vision 2020

- 5 years of universal primary education (I-V) to be achieved by 2007,
- Eight years of universal elementary (1-VIII) to be achieved by 2010,
- Twelve years of basic education (secondary and higher) to be achieved by 2020, and
- Achieving 75% literacy with at least 60% female literacy by the end of 2005 and universal literacy by 2010.

Steps Taken by Government of India

Constitutional Provisions

Education in the concurrent list (42nd constitutional Amendment, 1976). Equality before law (Art. 14). Education as a fundamental right (Art. 21A (93rd amendment). Discrimination against any citizen (Art. 15 (i). Special provision —(Art. 15 (3). Equality of opportunity in employment (Art. 16). Adequate means of livelihood (Art. 39 (a). Equal pay for equal work — (Art,39 (d). Free legal aid — (Art. 39 A). Maternity relief — (Art. 42). Promote educational & eco. Interest (Art.46). Standard of living and nutrition (Art.47). Protect the dignity of women (Art. 51 A (e). 1/3 of seats to be filled by direct election to be reserved for women (Art. 243 D (3).

Educational Provision

- NPE (1986) and Revised document (1992) emphasized the promotion of women's education.
- The National Commission for women was set up in 1990.
- The Government is working on the formulation of National Policy on women.
- The National Resource Center for women is proposed to be set up.
- Literacy has been a priority on the national agenda as a tool for social change.

What the Government have done for women so far

Dowry Prohibition Act is passed in 1961. Medical Termination of Pregnancy Act is passed in 1971. Child Marriage Restrict Act — 1976. Equal Remuneration Act—1976. Immoral Traffic (Prevention Act. Indecent Representation of Women (Prohibition) Act are passed in 1986. Commission of Sati, Prevention Act is passed in 1987,Prenatal Diagnostic Techniques (regulation and prevention of Misuse) Act was passed in 1992.

Specific Provisions have been incorporated in the constitution of India through the 73rd, 74th and 84th amendment Act with a view to empower and extend and enhance representation of women in Zilla Parisad, Block (Panchayat Samiti), village (Gram Panchayat) & Municipality /NAC, levels and in House of people in Parliament and in State Legislative Assemblies.

Other policies which advocates women's concern — National Plan of Action for women, 1976. National Perspective Plan for Women (1980-2000). National Policy for the empowerment of women (Draft) Plan of Action to combat commercial sexual exploitation of women and children.

Machineries — Both the Central and State Governments have set up Departments of Women and Child Development after 1985.

Support Services—Indira Mahila Yozana (IMY) hostels for working women. Mahila Samrudhi Yojana, (MSY). Support to Training & Employment Programme (STEP) for Women, Central Social Welfare Board (CSWB), (1953) — (12,000) V.Os, mainly in Tribal, rural and backward areas.

Institutes: National Institute of Public Co-operation and Child Development, (NIPCCD), National Commission for Women (NCW) is a Statutory Body set up under a Central Act in 1992.

The Commission strives for achieving equality and justice, through intervention in cases of violation of equality, deprivation of women's rights.

Programme initiatives: - 'Dahej- Mukta Abhijan' Prison Reforms for women under trials, Gender sensitizations workshops for the police, judiciary, doctors through training modules. Standing Commission for Empowerment of Women, Rashtriya Mahila Kosh (RMK)

Recommendations

- Literacy based on skills may be organized through women's self-help groups (SHGs) and Anganbadi Centre in the state.
- The learners should be encouraged to provide leadership.
- The pedagogy should be rooted in the culture and ethos of specific groups (SC/ST).
- Each district may have Jana Sikshan Sansthan (J.S.S.) for skill training & Jobs.

In spite of the above initiatives undertaken by the government, the gap between men and women in widening and thus the development of the whole nation is affected.

Time has come to review and rethink some alternative and innovative strategies. The issues of women need to be properly addressed. Concerted effort and initiatives need to be undertaken to meet the gender equality and holistic national development.

Rethinking Thrusts

(a) New Paradigms of Development

- It is time that the concept of women hood need to be viewed in the light of Vedic insight Women are the ardhanginis, equal sharer with men. According to the Eastern view men and women are complementary to each other. They can actualize their maximum potentialities and learn to live in harmony with themselves, laws of nature and development.

The western view of the concept of woman is an independent, more aggressive and more liberal partner of life on equal terms with man. The concept of complementarity and harmony is not so deeply rooted in their relationship.

Women must do a ruthless introspection into the cultural ethos of the country and the process of modernization and industrialization taking place and try to strike a delicate balance between the classical wisdom of the East and the scientific advances of the west. The present century poses threats and opportunities to human civilization and harmony of man-woman, man and nature. Hence the vision, perception, policies and programmes for women development call for a paradigm shift. From the dominance of male superiority to the concept of complementarity and harmony, from the narrow perception of reality to the holistic ecological paradigm of women development.

(b) New Role of Man

- No society can ever develop half liberated and half shackled. "Shabana Azmi said that inequality is inculcated in both men and women from birth, before they can think for themselves. "What we are overlooking is the role and responsibility of men and their attitudes which shape the views of women in most of our societies." A more positive, political, social and cultural environment must be fostered to promote changes in these attitudes towards women.

(c) Alleviation of Poverty

- Gender in-equality linked to poverty. Attention to need based vocational training and equality of opportunity on the labour market is fundamental for addressing the issues of poverty. Pakistan Government has adopted an integrated approach of linking primary education with nutrition health care, population, welfare, water supply and sanitation by the illiterate adult women and dropped out girls.

(d) Self Perception of Women and New Notion of Power

- We can say that the process of empowerment begins in the mind, from the awakening of a women's consciousness. Empowerment should generate new notions of power and pave the way for a 'more humane society for all'.

(e) *Feminism*

- Western parameters of women development are inconsistent with our cultural ethos. Indira Gandhi believed in the concept of complementarity between man and woman and wanted to evolve a new developmental model. Her perennial message for women was 'to strive, to seek to find and not to yield.'

(f) A System View of Life

- Paradigm shift in the philosophy, policies and programmes need to be emphasized. From the dominance of male superiority and polarities to the concept of complementarity from the fragmented and narrow perception of reality to a holistic and ecological paradigm of women development.

(g) Rise of Sensate Culture

- One wonders why did women who held a prominent position and excelled in various activities in Vedic times had forfeited their status, self-confidence and freedom during the medieval and British period. Some thinkers and social scientists have attributed the male dominance to the philosophy of pragmatism and the rise of sensate culture.

(h) Humanistic Role

- Women could emancipate the earth and ecosystem, they could give the message of 'Vasudheba Kutumbakam.' With their feminine qualities - Compassion, love and understanding which are urgently required to counter balance violence, conflict, tension and hatred among people and save the eco system from the tentacles of destruction.

(i) Helping Self (women)

- Women, must not expect complete freedom rather they should be least dependent on male members. Through knowledge and power can think of undertaking any task at par with men but not under them, may be with them. Thinking positive and becoming assertive with decency and dignity.

(j) Development Model

- It needs to be well founded on the rich Indian Culture values and ethics. Modernization can be attained through the development of inner cultural growth and outer role played by them conforming to Indian quality of life, vision and mission.

(k) Attitude and Mindsets of Women Towards other Women

- Just because a woman is educated or earning can she improve her status? The woman can earn money through her job she cannot buy, a saree or spend money without the permission of her mother in law. Unless the traditional, orthodox attitude of woman is changed towards other women the status of women will not enhance.

(l) Exhibitionism and Over Smartness

- Females like to show up and exhibit. It is because of undue smartness and ultra modern fashion and style over aggressive nature of women, which induce uncivilized lots to exploit them to any brutal extent.

  Dress, manners, dignity of women must be well rooted in our culture and values side by side their knowledge, skills and abilities and vision must be tuned with advancement of science and technology of the developed nation.

(m) Restricted use of Freedom

- Complete freedom may not be granted to women but women need to be less dependent on male counter parts for their sustenance and development.

Guidelines of the UNFPA

- Bring schools closer to the community and increase parent involvement.
- By providing tangible incentives. Incentives could include

the provision of scholarships, free distribution of textbooks provision of Mid day meals or stipend to parents.

- Change parents views towards the education of girls messages should stress that education enhances the income earning potential of young women.
- Design schools to fit the needs of girls. The Sikshya Karmi Project in Rajasthan, India succeeded in boosting girls enrolment in remote villages by running night schools.
- Increase the number of female teachers in general and more female teachers from Scheduled Tribe communities in areas dominated by tribals.
- Develop relevant curricula—In India school text books are being revised in order to eliminate gender biases. Dr Sadik underlined the value of adding population education to the curriculum that will combat gender discrimination. The National Curricular Frame work, 2005 also high lights that gender bias should be eliminated in text books and teaching learning process.

Linking learning to Poverty alleviation—The need of illiterate adult women and of girls (dropped outs) are best achieved through poverty alleviation programmes.

Development Model

Education is the prime mover of prosperity of a nation. It is the powerful instrument of silent social revolution and transformation. The initial step of education is literacy and awareness, Education is thus linked with the process of empowerment and empowerment of women leads to quality of life and ultimately brings National Development.

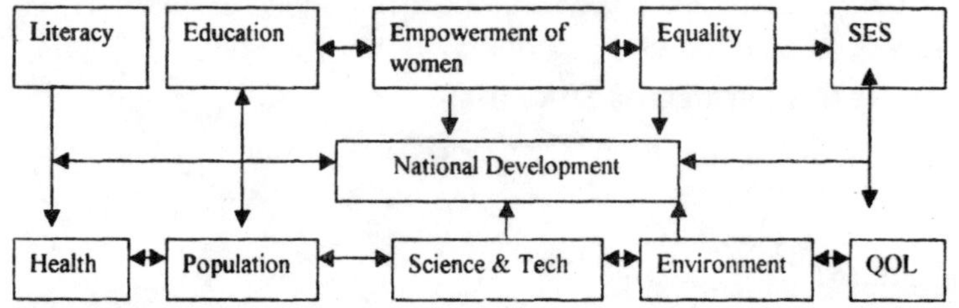

Shahnaz Wazir Ali spl. Asstt. for the P.M. for social sector said his government (Pakistan government) has adopted the integrated approach, Linking primary education with nutrition, health care, population welfare, rural water supply and sanitation. In India the

Mahila samakshya or Education for the Women's equality has achieved impressive result because of Mahila Sangha's at village level.

REFERENCES

Gandhi, Kishore (1992), *A New Episte..nology of Women Development : A focus on Complementarity,* Univ. News, Vol. XXX, No. 3, January 20.

Khandai, Hemanta (2001), *The Role of University in empowering Women*, University, News. Vol. 40, No. 35.

Sudhakar Rohini (2002), *Education of the Women,* University News, Vol. 40, No. 35.

Srivastav, Gauri (2006), *Women's Identity in the Indian Society : Educational Perceptions,* University News, Vol. 44, No. 24, June 12-18.

National Policy in Education, (1986), POA, Ministry & HRD, Department of Education.

Sapru, R. K. (1989), *Women & Development,* Ashis Publishing House, New Delhi,

EDUCATION AMONG THE WOMEN OF THE TRIBAL SOCIETY—Issues and Evidences

—RAJAN KU. SAHOO

Introduction

Education is a key to development. It is an effective tool not only for the upliftment of an individual but also for the society as a whole. Women constitute an important segment of the society and perform multiple roles as mothers, wives and daughters. Education is essential for them to prepare themselves for participation in development process from which they as well as the society will benefit. An educated mother enhances the literacy skill of' the family, provides better hygiene, increases the financial status imparting vocational education, conquers disadvantages, discrimination and fight against exploitation. So it is rightly said that if you educate a man, you educate an individual and if you educate a woman you educate a family. So when education of women is regarded as an important indicator of the development of the country, it is interesting to explore the level of literacy of women folk among Scheduled 'I'ribes' who are docile, simple honest, hardworking and hospitable but economically exploited, physically oppressed, socially ostracized humiliated, culturally isolated, politically unconscious and have little education to understand the issues in right perspective.

Objectives

Considering the importance of women education in tribal society the study was planned with following objectives.

- To study the level of women literacy in tribal society of India.

- To compare the level of literacy of tribal women with the literacy level of women of general and scheduled caste category.
- To find out various issues which stand on the way of the development of women education in tribal society.
- To suggest various policy measures for the development of education among the tribal women.

Methodology

The paper was prepared collecting information from various secondary sources. Various books, journals, research reports both of Govt. and Non-Government organizations have been consulted. Besides this the past experiences and observations which the researcher had gained while he was working in tribal areas have been incorporated to prepare the paper.

Education of Tribal Women in India

Education is one of the most important inputs for rapid socio-economic development of' the scheduled tribe people. But unfortunately tribal women who are regarded as economic assets and the principal bread earners of the family along with all the household chores fail to reap the benefit of the educational system. In the year 1961 the level of female literacy in Scheduled Tribe community was only 3.16 per cent which is very less to their counterparts who are members of General Category and Scheduled Caste communities. Their literacy rates in 1961 were 15.35 per cent and 3.29 per cent respectively. The figure is remarkably low when compared with the male members of their community as well as General and SC categories. The literacy rates of male members of ST, SC and General category were 13.83, 19.96 and 40.40 per cent respectively. Due to implementation of various policies for the development of education in general and women education in tribal society in particular, the rate of literacy of both males and females in ST, SC and General category both in rural and urban areas has increased in successive decades. Which has been given in Table No. 6.1 and Table No. 6.2 In 1991 the women literacy in tribal society has increased to 18.19 per cent from 3.16 per cent in 1961. Their counter parts among General and Scheduled Caste categories of people in percent term is 39.29 and 23.76. It is seen from these figures that the increase in literacy rate in case of General and Scheduled Caste women is proportionately more.

Similarly while the difference in literacy rate of male and female tribal people is 22.46 per cent it is 24.84 and 26.15 per cent among the General and Scheduled Caste communities.

Table 6.1 : Category wise break up of Literacy Rate in India during the Period from 1961 to 1991

(Literacy rate in per cent)

Census	*General*			*Scheduled Castes*			*Scheduled Tribe*		
	Person(s)	*Male*	*Female*	*Person(s)*	*Male*	*Female*	*Person(s)*	*Male*	*Female*
1961	28.30	40.40	15.35	10.27	16.96	3.29	8.53	13.83	3.16
1971	34.45	45.96	21.97	14.67	22.36	6.44	11.30	17.63	4.85
1981	43.57	56.38	29.76	21.38	31.12	10.93	16.35	24.52	8.04
1991	52.21	64.31	39.29	37.41	49.91	23.76	29.60	40.65	18.19

Sources (a) 1961, Census of India 1961: Part V A(i) Special Tribes for SC/ST.
(b) 1971 Paper I of 1975: Census of India 1971, SCs/STs Part VA(i).
(c) 1981: Census of India, 1981: PCA SCs/STs series I Part IB (ii) and B(iii) 1981.
(d) 1991: Census of India 1991, Final Popularion Totals (Paper 2 of 1992).

Table 6.2 : Category and Residence wise break up of Literacy Rates of Females during the period from 1961 to 1991

(Rate of literacy in per cent)

Census	*General*			*Scheduled Castes*			*Scheduled Tribe*		
	Rural	*Urban*	*Total*	*Rutal*	*Urban*	*Total*	*Rural*	*Urban*	*Total*
1961	10.10	40.50	15.35	2.52	10.04	3.29	2.90	13.45	2.90
1971	15.50	48.80	21.97	5.06	16.99	6.44	4.36	19.64	4.36
1981	21.70	56.30	29.76	8.45	24.34	10.93	6.81	27.32	6.81
1991	30.60	64.0	39.29	19.45	42.29	23.76	16.02	45.66	16.02

Sources (a) 1961, Census of India 1961: Part V A(i) Special Tribes for SC/ST.
(b) 1971 paper I of 1975: Census of India 1971, SCs/STs part VA(i).
(c) 1981: Census of India, 1981: PCA SCs/STs series I Part I B(ii) and B(iii) 1981.
(d) 1991: Census of India 1991, Final Population Totals (Paper 2 of 1992).

Similarly the literacy rate of tribal women in rural and urban areas depicted in Table 6.2 may be judged from various angles. In 1961 the literacy rate of tribal women in rural area was 2.90 per cent where as the rate in urban area was 13.45. In rural area (the literacy rate of SC and General Category women were 2.52 and 10.10 per cent respectively. This indicates that the scheduled caste women are lagging behind the scheduled tribe women in rural area. In urban area the literacy rates of the General and SC Category women were 40.50 and 10.04 per cent. Again that Scheduled Caste Women in urban area are lagging behind the Scheduled Tribe Women in literacy front. In 1991 the literacy rate of ST women in rural area has increased from 2.90 per cent to 16.02 per cent. The difference 13.12 is less than the difference in case of SCs and general categories of women which are 16.93 and 20.50 respectively. This reveals the fact that in rural literacy front the SCs and general category women have developed more during the twenty years. But in case of increase in literacy of urban tribal women, it is more in comparison to general category though it is slightly less than the SC category urban women. The difference between literacy rate of urban ST women is 32.21 during the period from 1961 to 1981 but it is 23.50 in case of general category and 32.25 in case of SC urban women.

The over all figure of literacy of the ST Women is low and their literacy status is significantly low in rural areas. 8 out of every 10 ST women are illiterate.

Emerging Issues

It is pertinent that the literacy rate of women in tribal society is very low. From the general observation and long association of the researcher with tribal people he draws inference that there are several emerging issues for which the women education in tribal society is lagging behind.

(i) More allocation of funds and opening of schools do not go far in providing education to the tribals. Formal education has not been necessary for the members of tribal societies to discharge their social obligations. Hence they should be prepared to accept education and it should be presented to them according to their suitability. The presentation of education should be in such a way as to cut the barriers of superstition and prejudice.

(ii) There is still a widespread feeling among the tribals that education makes their girl turn modern or go astray. Some tribal groups believe that their Gods shall be angry if they send their children to schools run by outsiders.

(iii) Since most of the tribal people are living in abject poverty under subsistence economy, it is not easy for most of them to send their children to schools.

(iv) In many states tribal children are taught through the same books which form the curriculum of non-tribal children of the urban and rural areas of the rest of the state. Obviously the content of such books rarely appeals to the tribal children who come from different cultural backgrounds.

National consciousness should not be imposed from above or outside, but they should be made aware of it, in a systematic manner.

(v) Education in India has spread in haphazard way without taking care of future needs. Tribal education also could not escape this anomaly and became instant failure due to apathy, indifference and lack of interest of the tribal people in formal education.

(vi) Under the traditional tribal set up a child enters adulthood with confidence. He knows his environment thoroughly, knows how to construct his own house, cultivate his field, weave his cloth; in short he acquires all the skills to lead a reasonably comfortable life within the limitations of his culture. The simple skill of reading and writing acquired in an over formal school is no match for this. We cannot afford to push him back to his environment naked. Therefore a balance should be struck somewhere to evolve a system of curricula where the tribal school, in addition to being a part of the national scheme, should have a supplementary curriculum adapted to the specific local conditions.

(vii) Certain tribal activities like agriculture, dancing, hunting, tribal games and archery must be allowed to find fullest expression in the extra-curricular activities of the school, thus providing some continuity of the traditional values and forms of organizations.

(viii) Lack of suitable teachers is one of the major reasons for the slow growth of education in tribal areas. Most of the teachers employed for imparting education to the tribal children show little appreciation of tribal way of life and value system. They approach tribal people with a sense of superiority and treat them as 'savage and uncivilized' and hence fail to establish proper rapport with their students.

(ix) A teacher in tribal area must have a thorough knowledge of tribal life and culture. He must speak tribal language. Only so can he be in a position to act as a friend, philosopher and guide to the tribal people.

(x) One of the major problems in tribal education is that of language. Most of the tribal languages and dialects are in the most rudimentary stage and there is hardly any written literature. Most of the states impart education to tribal and non-tribal children alike through the medium of the regional language which makes the education uninteresting and also hurts tribal sentiments.

(xi) Most of the tribal villages are scattered. This entails long travels to attend schools. Unless the school is situated very close to their villages and its site approved by the local people, the result especially for girls shall not be encouraging.

(xii) School building also plays an important role in growth of education among the tribal folk. Due to mismanagement, bungling and sometimes financiai constraints, the building is seldom suitable to run an educational institution.

(xiii) Most of the primary schools run in tribal areas are single teacher managed whose presence in the school is more an exception than a rule.

(xiv) The enthusiasm of tribal people in the education of their children also depends considerably on the timing of school hours in different seasons, It should not class with their important socio economic activities and events.

(xv) Domestic duties, employment at home and outside create an impediment to girls' access to education. She is often assigned the duty to look after the younger members of the family, as her mother has to work hard to add to the family income.

(xvi) The problem of absenteeism is a serious one in tribal areas. One sees a large number of students on the rolls but the actual attendance is really low and the number of students passing out at the final examinations is even lower.

On the basis of the emerging issues the researcher has prescribed the following suggestions for the development of Women Education in tribal society of our country.

(i) Blind believes and social taboos should be eliminated through various exhibitions, gatherings and announcements. Non-formal type of schooling should be developed for them which should not class with their seasonal operations.

(ii) Attitude of parents, and community as a whole should be effectively changed by village elites, officials and mass medias as a consequence of which girl students or women should be treated in equal footing without any discrimination.

(iii) Girl students should be given dresses, textbooks free of cost and scholarships or stipend on poor and meritorious ground as a consequences of which poverty will not stand on their way of educational development.

(iv) Tribal curriculum should be developed on the basis of their need and environment. Their education should start with the teaching of demography, history and ecology of their own region, their neighbourhood and state. They should be taught those vocations which will help them for earning their bread.

(v) Teachers with dedication and curiosity in tribal culture and traditional values should he posted in tribal areas. Such teachers should be given preference in promotion and rewarded in special occasions.

(vi) Teachers posted in tribal areas should be given training to learn tribal language and dialects. Sufficient tribal literature should be developed and students should be given education in their local language.

(vii) Schools should be opened in every village so distance of school will not be a problem for girl students. Government should extend sufficient care for the construction of an attractive school building.

(viii) Steps should be taken by the government to ensure regular attendance of teachers in schools. ICDS and creachs should be sufficiently opened as a consequence of which a girl can attend the school and burden of rearing up of siblings will not fall on her.

(ix) Parents should be motivated to make their children educated. So absenteeism will not be a regular feature in the schools.

Conclusion

While the legislative reformative, health and employment strategies have given Indian women a significant boost in their struggle for equal rights in the society, a lot is yet to be done in terms of giving them enough confidence to carry this struggle further. Not only do they have to fight against the age old bias, they also have to develop their own personality and capabilities against all odds as they have to maintain the social equilibrium and are the nerve centre of not only the Indian value system but also the guiding factor to our future generations. Education being the most effective instrument of empowering the Socially Disadvantaged Groups all our efforts should be made to improve the educational status of these groups. Closely associated with the well being of not only half of our population but also on the future of the country as a whole, because the well being of women alone can ensure the well being of our future generations.

REFERENCES

1. Bhutani Smita and Viveka Nagpal, *Dynamics of Rural Literacy in India,* University News, Association of Indian Universities, AIU House, 16 Comrade Indrajit Gupta Marg (Kotla Marg), New Delhi - 110002, Vol. 43, No. 20, May 16-22, 2005, pp.5-i6.
2. Dashora Rakesh and Anushree Sharma, *Role of Tribal Women in Education,* Yojana, Director, Publications Division, Ministry of Information and Broadcasting, Patiala House, New Delhi-110001, Vol 47, June, 2003, pp. 40-43.
3. Jayanthi C. *Role of Education and Social Change,* Yojana, Director Publication Division, Ministry of Information and Broadcasting, Patiala House, New Delhi- 110001, Vol. 47, No. 3, March 2003, pp. 15-17.
4. Khan Mohsin Ali, *Women's Education: Still a distant Dream,* Yojana, Director Publication Division, Ministry of Information and Board Casting Patial House, New Delhi-110001, Vol 45, December, 2001, pp. 40-43.
5. Kumar Akshay, *Equality of Women and the Social Mindset,* Employment News, Director Publication Division, Ministry of Information and Broadcasting, East Block-IV, Level —V, R.K. Puram, New Delhi 110066, Vol. XXVI, No. 48, March 28, 2002, pp. 1-3.
6. Mohanty, P.K.. *Tribal Education in India,* Employment News, Director Publication Division, Ministry of Information and Broadcasting, East Block IV, Level-5, R.K.Puram, New Delhi-110066, Vol. XXVIII, No. 38, December 20-26, 2003, pp. 1-3.
7. Sahoo, R.K, *Tribal Development in India,* Mohit Publications, 4675/21, Ansari Road, Daryaganj, New Delhi —110002, 2005.
8. Sekhar Madhu R., *Girls Education : Opening the Window on to the World,* Yojana, Director, Publication Division, Ministry of Information and Broadcasting, Patiala House, New Delhi- 110001, Vol. 45 November, 2001, pp. 46-47.
9. Senapati Tilottama, *Women Education in India: Emerging Issues and Outlook,* Souvenir, Silver Jubilee Edition, All Orissa Education Society, Bhubaneswar, 2005.

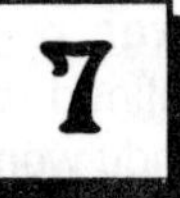

GENDER DISPARITY IN EDUCATION —Issues and Challenges

—KALPALATA PATRI

A woman feels keenly, thinks as clearly, as a man, she in her sphere does work as useful as a man does in his own. She has as much right to her freedom - to develop her personality to the full—as a man has. When she marries, she does not become the husband's servant but his equal partner. If his work is more important in the life of the community, her's is more important in the life of the family. Neither can do without the other. Neither is above the other or under the other. They are equals.

Lord Denning (1980)

Introduction

Women constitute the most elegant resource of a society and is the dynamic source of power. She comprises the very backbone of the family with multiple role - players of a mother, a wife, a pretty sister and a host of others. The status of a nation, its overall socio-economic condition can very well be assessed by judging and appraising the status of its women. From this point of view education plays an important role for providing educational opportunities for all. Education has been of central significance to the development of human society. Major emphasis has been laid on promoting equality through educating different classes, races, ethinic groups and castes. Gradually gender added a new dimension to this education-equality paradigm. It is being argued that equality among human beings could be achieved by providing opportunities for better health and education to girls and women.

Historical Background

During Vedic era there was a golden period so far as liberty/equality and dignity of Aryan women are concerned. Gradually the status was deteriorated and declined. The women could not enjoy independent status and was regarded as subservient and appendage to male and confined to household chores and child bearing. The conditions of Hindu women deteriorated further during medieval period. To safeguard fidelity and chastity of the women, she was deprived of education and confined to the four-walls of the house. Child marriage, *purdha pratha* and *sati pratha* became common. During British rule, social reformers like Raja Ram Mohan Rai and Dayananda Saraswati tried hard to eradicate those social evils.

Present Status

Independent India adopted the constitution and conferred various fundamental rights to all Indian irrespective of race, religion and sex Article-14 ensures "equality before law" and Article-15 "Prohibits any discrimination". The constitution also promises - social and economic justice to women. The Universal declaration on human right was also adopted and it is the endeavour of the central and state Government. to ensure human rights of individual and to curb violation of human right. In order to bridge the gap of Male-Female disparity every year in 8th March, International Women Day is celebrated. To make this notion more fruitful, India celebrated the year 2001 as the National Women Empowerment year. Those are the important landmarks in the context of women education.

A Closing but Persistent Gender Gap in Education

Despite of various efforts made at Governmental level the disparity in Gender is worth mentioning. Today the condition of women is very pitiable in rural areas. In a patriarchal society women are in a subordinate position, the symbol of fun and entertainment. In the orthodox society female child is considered a liability and male child is considered as a property. The National level picture as well as the State level picture regarding sex ratio is very gloomy and miserable.

State level picture presents the proportion of females consistently improved during the first 20 years of the present century. It rose from 1037 in 1901 to 1056 in 1911 and finally to 1086 in 1921. But from 1921, a downward curve in the ratio of females to males began and a decline trend is perceived (Fig. 7.2).

Table 7.1 : Sex Ratio (1901-2001)

(Females per 1000 male)

Years	*India*	*Orissa*
1901	972	1037
1911	964	1056
1921	955	1086
1931	950	1067
1941	945	1053
1951	946	1022
1961	941	1001
1971	930	988
1981	934	981
1991	927	970
2001	933	972

Source: "Census of India–2001, Series–1 India"
"Census of India–1991 Series–19 (Orissa)"

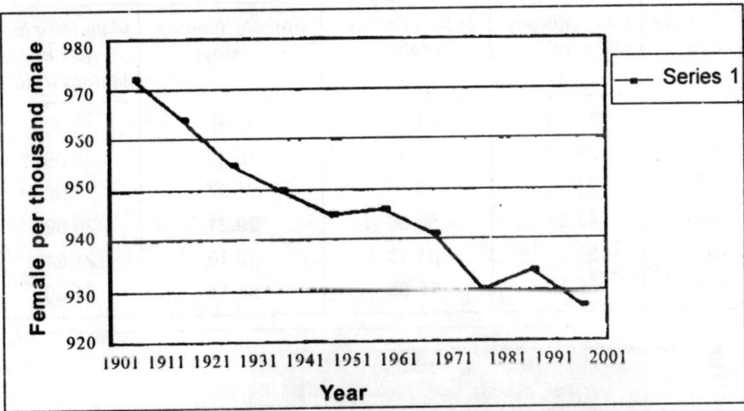

Fig. 7.1 : Sex Ratio Representing National Level (India) Picture (1901-2001)

National level picture presents a decline trend till 1991 (Fig. 7.1). This disparity in sex-ratio is very alarming. The reason for this may be assigned to the negligence of girl child, destruction of female foetus by advance detection etc.

A comparison can be drawn between the male and female literacy rates since 1951 to 2001. In India, while we have made progress in educating people, it is far from satisfactory. What is even more disturbing is that for women the situation is worse than that for men as reflected in literacy rates. (Table-7.2)

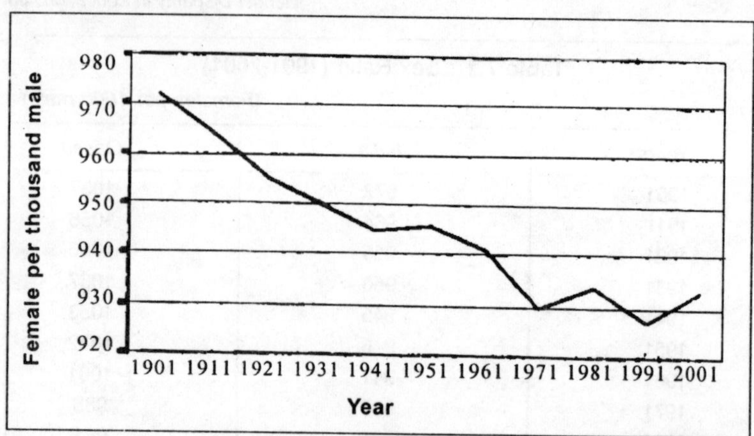

Fig. 7.2 : Sex Ratio Representing State Level ORRISA Picture (1901-2001)

Table 7.2 : Comparison of Literacy Rate between male and Female in India (1951-2001) (In terms of percentage)

Census Year	*Total Literacy rate*	*Male Literacy rate*	*Female literacy rate*	*Male-female gap in literacy rate*
1951	18.33	27.16	8.86	18.30
1961	28.30	40.40	15.35	20.05
1971	34.45	45.96	21.97	23.98
1981	43.57	56.96	29.21	26.62
1991	52.21	64.13	39.16	24.84
2001	65.38	75.85	54.16	21.69

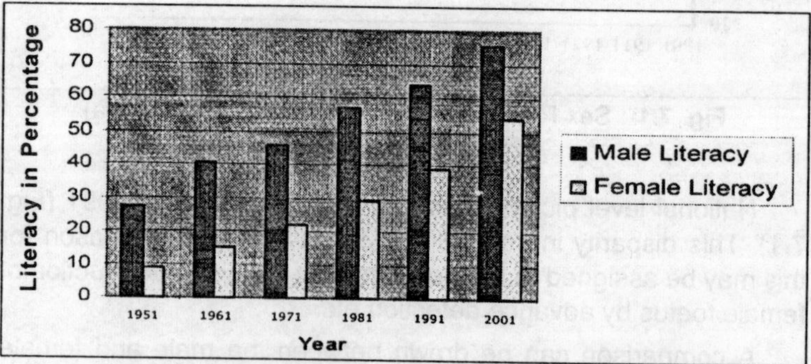

Fig. 7.3 : Disparity in Literacy Rate between Male and Female in India (1951-2001)

Source: Economic Survey Government of India, 2003-04.

Table - 7.2 portrays the literacy rates of India for the last five decades which suggest that the comprehensive education policies of the Government of India undertaken over the last few decades have been able to give a fillip to trigger the women's literacy rate in India. It is evident from the above data that since after independence the overall literacy rate of India has been highest during the decade 1991-2001. (65.38 per cent in 2001 as against 52.21 per cent in 1991 showing an increase of 13.17% over the last decade) For the first time the country witnessed a faster growth in female literacy i.e. 15.0 percentage point (54.16% in 2001 as against 39.16 per cent in 1991) which is higher than the increase in the male literacy rate of 11.7 percentage point. (75.85 per cent in 2001 as against 64.13 per cent in 1991). Although the percentage of educated male and female were increased yet the idea that the women have to be treated at par with men in the field of education could not be achieved. Even after fifty ninth year of independence, there still exists a great disparity between the male and female educational status (Fig. 7.3).

Likewise the national level figure, the state level picture indicates steady growth in the literacy rate since 1951 (Fig. 7.4). For the first time, the country witnessed a faster growth in female literacy that is 21.68 percentage point (50.51 in 2001 as against 28.83 per cent in 1991). No consistent trend is observed regarding the gender gap in Literacy. The female literacy in Orissa has grown almost twelve fold since 1951. Though it has grown from 4.52% to 50.51% since 1951-2001 but the gender gap pertaining to literacy has been increased from 23.58 per cent in 1991 to 24.84 per cent in 2001,

Table 7.3 : Literacy rate in Orissa (1951-2001) (In terms of Percentage)

Census Year	*Total Literacy*	*Male Literacy*	*Female Literacy*	*Male-female gap in Literacy*
1951	15.80	27.32	4.52	22.80
1961	21.66	36.48	8.65	27.83
1971	26.18	38.29	13.92	24.37
1981	34.23	47.10	21.12	25.98
1991	40.80	52.41	28.83	23.58
*2001	63.08	75.35	50.51	24.84

Source: "General Population Tables Part-II" Census of India-1951-2001 series 19 (Orissa)"

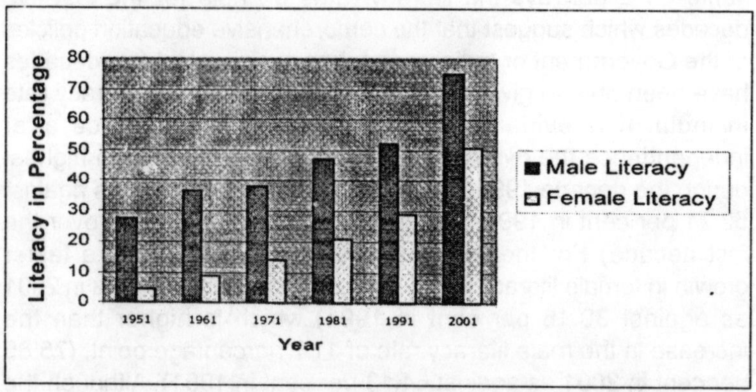

Fig. 7.4 : Disparity in Literacy Rate in Male and Female in Orissa (1951-2001)

registering an increase of 5.34 percentage point in 2001 over 1991. Both national as well as state level figure is gloomy and dismal in relation to gender gap pertaining to literacy. Besides literacy gap the decline trend in sex ratio puts serious thinking among the intellectual mass and the member of country to analyze the issues pertaining to gender gap.

Issues

In the under developed, developing countries female child is considered a liability and male child is considered as property. A female child is unwanted due to the fact that so many social difficulties are experienced in their bringing up, in educating, in providing job and getting them married. For this deteriorating condition of women the causes are of various types.

Economic Factor

The economic condition of the family prevents many parents from sending their girls to school. The families living below poverty line are not able to afford the high cost of education. In the critical situation they prefer to send their sons to school rather than their daughter.

Socio – Cultural Factor

The low status of women is a major factor hindering girls enrolment and retention. The custom of early marriage and non availability of girls school creates hindrance for its effective implementation. Since most of the societies are male oriented and male dominated, community and parental attitude towards girls education count a lot in decisions affecting sons education. When the question arises as to who should be educated fast, boy or girl the boy almost always comes up as the first choice when the question of who should drop out first comes, most often it is the girl.

Illiteracy of Parents

Parents education is strongly associated with the educational participation of girl. The study concluded that predisposition of the household towards promoting girl education is greatly enhanced by exposure of family members to formal education as well as to job which require higher level of education and training.

Psychological Factor

Girls, because of low status accorded to them by community and their parents, are bound to have low self esteem and would perceive themselves as inferior to boys. Their motivation for schooling is very low. Since their parents are ignorant or do not see the benefit of education for girl, they are unlikely to receive parental support.

Physical Environment of School

By reason of geography and topography, schools sometimes are at a considerable distance from the homes of the girls. Going to schools becomes inconvenient for the young children, especially girls. Long distance between school and home poses series problems for both young child as well as the older girls to attend school. Some times infrastructural facilities are inadequate to meet the need of girl child.

Shortage/Lack of Female Teachers

In a tradition bound society, preference for female teachers has been a recurring note. Non availability of women teacher creates harassness for the progress of women education. Parents feel more comfortable when their girls are under the care of female teachers. While the crucial need for women teachers has been identified and found essential, the problem lies in the availability of trained women teachers. Lack of women teachers create hindrance for the progress of women education.

Irrelevant Curriculum

Generally the school curriculum has been described as being irrelevant to the need of girls. In some cases, it is so urban-oriented that rural girls feel even more alienated.

Religious Factor

In our society male child is supposed to be a must for the salvation of the family. This factor motivates the parents to be blessed with a son rather than daughter, Not only that, parents spend their time and money in favour of establishing their son.

Cost Benefit Analysis by Parents

Of late when education has become very costly parents of girl child think that if they invest for the education of their male child the return will directly go to them in future. If the female child is educated and employed the money she will earn will go to the in-laws family. By making this analysis parents in some societies prefer the education of male child.

Challenges

There is urgent need not only to understand the importance of women's education but also to take effective measures towards addressing it, though it is a basic human right, In this context following challenges are to be seriously thought of for dreaming a better India.

Provision of School in all Areas

The state should continue to help in an abundant measure in providing necessary schooling facilities in all the areas and in all habitations, however small, so that the local population can make use of them.

Appointment of Women Teachers

The question of shortage of teachers is bound to remain for a long time and therefore, concerted effort have to be made to recruit as many women teachers as possible. It should be the aim of all states to appoint women teacher in primary schools and great number of women teacher in mixed school.

School Improvement Conferences

School improvement conferences should be arranged widely throughout the states and particularly in the less advanced states in order to encourage people to contribute to educational awakening and advancement.

School Building

The existing functional deficiencies of schools should be remedied by replacing buildings which are totally inadequate to modern educational needs. There should be appropriate building with other infrastructural facilities for meeting the need of girl child.

Awareness Programme

Different awareness Programmes should be organized by different agencies for holding legal literacy programme for making women aware of laws relating to women and gender discrimination. Besides health awareness, environmental education and population education be imparted for developing their consciousness to different issues.

Organization of Self Help Group (SHG)

Efforts must be made at various level for motivating women to form SHGS. These groups will receive loans from banks for undertaking various income generating activities. This may facilitate the economic condition of the family.

Literacy Activities

Women literacy and basic skills project should form an important nonformal educational programme for the poor and rural women. In addition to functional literacy the women should be trained in important life skills related activities.

Conclusion

Education is considered a key instrument of change to abolish this evil of gender discrimination. It is true to saying","If you educate a boy" you educate an individual, but if you educate a girl you educate a family' society and ultimately the nation. Education liberates women from ignorance and enhance herself esteem. It enables them to choose their own way and look after their families in a better way. Besides, education can change the social attitude of the people in positive perspective. To quote Napoleon Bonaparte who has rightly said "Give me an educated mother, I shall promise you the birth of civilized nation.

REFERENCES

Taj, Haseen, (2005), *Current Challenges in Education,* Hyderabad; Neel Kamal Publication Pvt. Ltd.

Walia, J.S., (2002), *Modern Indian Education and its Problems.* Jalandhar; Paul Publishers.

Sharma, Santosh, (2004), Pseudo Gender Equality and the Empowerment of Women, *University News*, Vol - XLII, pp. 5-9.

Srivastava, Nalini, (2005), Empowerment of Women through Higher Education, *University News*, Vol. - XL III, pp. 131-138.

8

ILLITERACY OF WOMEN IN RURAL INDIA AND THE CALL OF NATION FOR DEVELOPMENT

—Tilottama Senapati

Introduction

Literacy rate of an area is infact the indicator of its level of socio-economic development. Raising of literacy level of India especially the female literacy will undoubtedly contribute immensely towards alleviating poverty, reducing infant mortality rate, improving public health, protecting environment, strengthening human rights, helping to improve international understanding etc. When a man is educated an individual is educated but when an woman is educated the family is educated. So women education has an important role in the developmental process of a nation. But in a country where illiteracy still dominates better not to say any thing about women literacy and in such a situation expecting the development of a nation is futile. So in the formulation of education policies of the country, removal of illiteracy especially of women must be the central and primary object. India is a country of villages. Gandhiji was rightly worried, "If villages perish, India also perishes". So Gandhiji wanted to develop the villages. For the development of rural India development of education of a rural woman is essential. So when India is passing through a critical stage of development, it is worth while to study the status of women literacy in rural India.

Objectives

Considering the importance of literacy of rural women for the development of nation, the study was planned with the following objectives:

- To study the status of literacy among rural women in india.
- To study the extent of difference in literacy rate between female and male at rural and urban level.
- To focus in brief the causes of illiteracy among the rural women in India.
- To prescribe suitable policy measures to counter the problems of illiteracy which will subsequently help for the development of literacy among women in rural areas.

Methodology

The paper was prepared collecting information from secondary sources. Various books journals, research papers both from published and non-published sources of Govt. and Non-government organizations have been consulted.

Status of Literacy of Rurai Women in India

The Ministry of Human Resource Development and the Planning Commission decided that the literacy rate be worked out only for the aged seven and above. It is an important fact that while the number of literate males in 1991 census was significantly higher than that of the illiterate males, illiteracy continued to reign among females. The number of illiterate females in 1991 census exceeded that of literate females by 70 million.

The 2001 census recorded a literacy rate of 65.2 per cent in India while it is 75. 64 per cent in case of' males it is 54.03 per cent for females, The most significant feature of the 2001 census was that for the first time in the demographic history of the country the number of female literates exceeded that of female illiterates. During the period more female literates (226.757 million) were recorded than female illiterates (192.997 million) though the number of illiterate rural females (161.024 million) continued to exceed the number of literate rural females (140.398 million) (census of India 2001).

The issue is of a great concern as more than 70 per cent of India's total population lives in rural areas. It is further more heart burning as more than 250 million villagers are still illiterate. In contrast with rural female literacy of only 46.58 per cent the rural male literacy in 2001 was 71.18 per cent. The number of illiterate females in rural areas is a matter of still great concern. Their number exceeded 160 million as against a total of approximately 140 million literate rural females.

The rural urban difference in literacy is more pronounced in case of women than for men. Among the rural female population in the age group of 7 years and above, the literacy rate is 46.58 per cent against 72.99 per cent among the urban female population. The corresponding figures for rural and urban male population on other hand are 71.18 per cent and 86.42 per cent respectively.

Both gender and residential differentials in the female literacy rate vary considerably both in the country as well as across the states and union territories which has been shown in the Table 8.1.

The table shows that in 2001 census the general female literacy rate is lower than the male literacy rate in the country as well as across the states and union territories. However though in the states like Kerala, Mizoram, Goa, Maharastra, Himachal Pradesh, Tripura, Tamil Nadu, Punjab, Nagaland, Sikkim, Meghalaya, Uttaranchal, West Bengal, Manipur, Karnataka, Haryana, Assam, Gujarat and Union Territories like Lakshadweep, A &N Islands, Delhi, Pondichery, Daman & Diu the female literacy is higher than the National average (53.03%). It is lower in Union Territory, Dadra and Nagar Haveli and states like Chhatisgarh, Andhra Pradesh, Orissa, Madhya Pradesh, Rajasthan, Arunachal Pradesh, Uttar Pradesh, J & K, Jharkhand and Bihar.

Similarly the Male-Female urban literacy is higher than the male-female rural literacy in all the states and Union Territories. The literacy rate of rural males is more than the rural females is seen in every state and Union Territory of the country. The female literacy of rural areas in states like Kerala, Mizoram, Goa, Maharastra, Himachal Pradesh, Tripura, Tamilnadu, Punjab, Nagaland, Sikkim, Meghalaya, Uttaranchal, West Bengal, Manipur, Karnataka, Haryana, Assam, Chhatishgarh, Orissa and Union Territories Lakshadweep, Chandigarh, A & N Islands, Delhi, Pondicherry, Daman & Diu is more than the National Average (46.58%) but it is lower in Union Territory Dadra and Nagar Haveli and states like Gujarat, Andhra Pradesh, Madhya Pradesh, Rajasthan, Arunachal Pradesh, Uttar Pradesh, J & K, Jharkhand and Bihar.

The ratio between urban and rural literates which was 2.86: 1.00 in 1951 has got reduced to 1.35:1 .00 in 2001. The contrasts have been sharper in urban-rural female literate ratio than urban rural male literate ratio since 1951 till 2001 as shown in Table 8.2.

Table 8.1 : Female Literacy Rate in India by Gender and Residence, 2001

(Literacy Rate by Per cent)

Sl. No.	India/ State/ Union/ Territory	Literacy Rate					
		Persons		In Rural		In Urban	
		Male	Female	Male	Female	Male	Female
	India	75.64	54.03	71.18	46.58	86.42	72.99
1.	Kerala	94.20	87.86	93.54	86.79	96.07	90.87
2.	Mizoram	90.69	86.13	84.38	76.17	96.97	95.69
3.	Goa	88.88	75.51	87.69	71.55	90.06	79.65
4.	Maharashtra	86.27	67.51	82.17	59.12	91.42	79.25
5.	Himachal Pradesh	84.57	67.08	83.58	65.23	91.49	85.91
6.	Tripura	81.47	65.41	78.89	61.05	93.51	85.36
7.	Tamilnadu	82.33	64.55	77.47	55.84	88.40	75.64
8.	Punjab	75.63	63.55	71.70	57.91	82.97	74.63
9.	Nagaland	71.77	61.92	67.73	57.87	89.01	82.09
10.	Sikkim	76.73	61.46	75.11	59.05	88.61	80.19
11.	Meghalaya	66.14	60.41	59.90	54.02	89.90	84.30
12.	Uttaranchal	84.01	60.26	82.74	55.52	87.21	74.77
13.	West Bengal	77.58	60.22	73.75	53.82	86.49	76.14
14.	Manipur	77.87	59.70	74.50	55.88	88.72	71.47
15.	Karnataka	76.29	57.45	70.63	48.50	86.58	74.87
16.	Haryana	79.25	56.31	76.13	49.77	86.58	72.05
17.	Assam	71.93	56.03	69.02	52.25	89.88	81.03
18.	Gujarat	76.46	55.61	70.71	45.75	85.46	72.23
19.	Chhatisgarh	77.86	52.28	74.58	47.41	89.87	71.63
20.	Andhra Pradesh	70.85	51.17	66.13	44.36	83.21	69.34
21.	Orissa	75.95	50.97	73.57	47.22	88.32	72.68
22.	Madhya Pradesh	76.50	50.55	72.10	42.96	87.78	70.62
23.	Rajasthan	76.46	44.34	72.96	37.74	87.10	65.42
24.	Arunachal Pradesh	54.74	44.24	64.07	37.56	85.61	70.60
25.	Uttar Pradesh	70.23	42.97	68.01	37.74	78.13	62.05
26.	Jammu & Kashmir	65.75	41.82	60.34	35.09	80.30	62.22
27.	Jharkhand	67.94	39.38	59.90	30.33	87.73	70.71
28.	Bihar	60.32	33.57	57.70	30.03	80.80	63.30
	Union Territories						
1.	Lakshadweep	93.15	81.56	92.56	79.86	93.85	83.60
2.	Chandigarh	85.65	76.65	81.54	67.17	86.16	77.53
3.	Andaman & Nicobar Islands	86.07	75.29	83.90	72.23	90.35	81.65
4.	Delhi	87.37	75.00	87.15	68.23	87.38	75.49
5.	Pondicherry	88.89	74.13	83.87	64.63	91.40	78.78
6.	Daman & Diu	88.40	70.37	86.48	63.31	92.72	79.14
7.	Dadra & Nagar Haveli	73.32	42.99	67.13	34.08	91.57	75.67

Source: Census of India, 2001, Series-I, India, Provisional Population Totals, 2001.

Table 8.2 : India-Urban Rural Literacy Rates and Ratios 1951-2001

Year	*Males*	*Urban-Rural male Literature Ratio*	*Females*	*Urban-Rural Female Literate Ratio*	*Persons*	*Urban-rural Literate Ratio*
1951	–	2.40:1.00	–	4.58:1.00	–	2.86:1.00
Rural	19.02	–	4.87	–	12.10	–
Urban	45.60	–	22.33	–	34.59	–
Total	27.16	–	8.86	–	18.33	–
1961	–	1.92:1.00	–	4.01:1.00	–	2.42:1.00
Rural	34.30	–	10.10	–	22.50	–
Urban	66.00	–	40.50	–	54.40	–
Total	40.40	–	15.35	–	28.30	–
1971	–	1.44:1.00	–	3.15:1.00	–	2.16:1.00
Rural	48.60	–	15.50	–	27.90	–
Urban	69.80	–	48.80	–	60.20	–
Total	45.96	–	21.97	–	34.45	–
1981	–	1.55:1.00	–	2.59:1.00	–	1.87:1.00
Rural	49.60	–	21.70	–	36.00	–
Urban	76.70	–	56.30	–	67.20	–
Total	56.38	–	29.76	–	43.57	–
1991	–	1.40:1.00	–	2.09:1.00	–	1.64:1.00
Rural	57.90	–	30.60	–	44.70	–
Urban	81.10	–	64.00	–	73.10	–
Total	64.13	–	39.29	–	52.21	–
2001	–	1.21:1.00	–	1.57:1.00	–	1.35:1.00
Rural	71.40	–	46.70	–	59.40	–
Urban	86.70	–	73.20	–	80.30	–
Total	75.85	–	54.16	–	65.38	–

Source: Census of India, 2001.

Urban-rural female literate ratio has experienced continuous decline since 1951 and it has come down from 4.58:1.00 in 1951 to 1.57:1.00 in 2001 while the urban-rural male literacy ratio has come down from 2.40:1.00 to 1.21:1.00 during the period from 1951 to 2001.

Similarly among scheduled tribe population the urban-rural differential in female population has registered most impressive progress. This differential between rural urban areas has been reduced from 4.64:1.00 in 1961 to 2.85:1.00 in 1991 which has been shown in Table No. 8.3.

Table 8.3 : India: Literacy Rates of Females of Scheduled Caste and Scheduled Tribe Population of India by Residence during the period from 1961-1991

(Literacy Rate in Per cent)

Census year	*Scheduled Caste Population*			*Urban Rural SC*	*Scheduled Tribe Population*			*Urban Rural ST*
	Total	*Rural*	*Urban*	*Literature*	*Total*	*Rural*	*Urban*	*Literature*
1961(a)	3.29	2.52	10.04	3.98:1.00	3.16	2.90	13.45	4.64:1.00
1971(b)	6.44	5.06	16.99	3.36:1.00	4.85	4.36	19.64	4.50:1.00
1981(c)	10.93	8.45	24.35	2.88:1.00	8.04	6.81	27.32	4.01:1.00
1991(d)	23.76	19.45	42.29	2.17:1.00	18.19	16.02	45.66	2.85:1.00

Sources: (a) 1961: Census of India 1961: Part VA(i) Special Tables for SC/ST.
(b) 1971: Paper 1 of 1975: Census of India 1971, SCs/STs Part VA(i)
(c) 1981: Census of India 1981: PCA SC/STs series 1 part 1 B(ii) & B(iii) 1981.
(d) 1991: Census of India 1991: Final Population Totals (Paper 2 of 1992).

In 1961 the literacy rate of ST females in rural area was 2.90 per cent while it was 13.45 per cent is urban area. In 1991 the female literacy rate among ST has become 16.02 per cent in rural area while in urban area it has increased to 45.66 per cent.

In case of Scheduled Caste population, the urban-rural differential in female population has been reduced from 3.98:1.00 to 2.17:1.00. which has been shown in Table No. 8.3 In 1961 the literacy rate of Scheduled Caste females in rural areas was 2.52 while it was 10.04 per cent in urban area. The per cent of literacy among females (SC) both in rural and urban areas have improved to 9.45 per cent and 42.29 per cent respectively.

Causes of Low Female Literacy Rate in Rural Area

It is obvious from the figure presented above that there is low female literacy in rural area. There are several causes for low female literacy rate in rural area of the country.

(i) The urban-rural gap in literacy is attributed to appalling poverty in rural areas even when education is free. There are many costs for attending a school, including uniforms, textbooks, and participation in social activities of the school.

(ii) One of the principal reasons which keeps many girls out of the schools system especially in the rural areas is that they are required to work at a very young age in various domestic chores. They collect firewood, fetch water from near and far, take ,food and water to parents in their places of work, look after their younger siblings besides being responsible for many other activities. Many are compelled to work either as paid or unpaid workers. Therefore, being in school implies foregoing the opportunities to earn or help in the home. For the poor the immediate costs of income lost and results are often too high.

(iii) The number of schools in the rural areas has been inadequate. The availability of schools has not increased in proportion in which the population has increased. The majority of the primary schools do not have adequate facilities. Forty four per cent of the primary schools in the country do not have pucca buildings and 59.5 per cent don't have drinking water, Moreover as many as 89 per cent of the primary schools, 70 per cent of the middle and 27 per cent of the secondary schools in the rural areas don't have toilets.

(iv) Villagers hesitate in sending their children to distantly located schools.

(v) The co-education could be held responsible for the withdrawal and non-participation of a considerable number of girls. Schools exclusively for girls have for long been argued as an essential ingredient for enhancing female participation in the Indian setting. Lack of separate girls' school has been handicap in education of girl students.

(vi) Another factor contributing to denial of education to girls is the lack of female teachers in villages. Despite the recommendations of several commissions e.g. Education Commission (1964-66) for a rapid expansion in the number of women teachers and their suggestions regarding the provision of special allowances and accommodation to attract female teachers in rural areas only 28.8 per cent of all teachers are female.

(vii) Literate rural folk also tend to migrate to urban areas for better prospects, there by reducing the proportion of rural literates and increasing the proportion of urban illiterates.

(viii) The formal educational system eludes many children, especially those who have to work for a living, either on paid or unpaid basis. Girls constitute a significant proportion of these child workers. It would be extremely necessary that the curriculum be practical and work oriented and based on the needs and the interests of the girls.

Panaceas for Correcting the ills of Low Female Literacy in Rural Area

Considering the various causes of low female literacy the following policy measures may be undertaken to correct the ills.

(i) Sufficient financial provision should be made in form of stipend or scholarship to the students, provision for uniform and text books free of cost for effectively fighting against appalling poverty of the students.

(ii) Pre-school and crèches should be sufficiently opened to free the girl children from rearing up of siblings and household chores.

(iii) Adequate schools should be opened in every village so that distance of school will not be hindrance for the development of literacy of rural females.

(iv) Separate institutions should be opened for girl children and the women teachers should be exclusively appointed there.

(v) The non-formal education (NFE) programme introduced in the government in 1979 in nine educationally backward states aimed at providing relevant and need based education to out of school children between the ages 9 to 14.

(vi) Wide urban rural difference in literacy needs to be narrowed down by strengthening the rural—urban interaction, greater diversification of rural economy and awakening particularly of rural females.

(vii) Decreasing size of land holding in rural areas has its own impact on rural literacy. It results in the village folk seeking avenues of livelihood other than dependence on agriculture. Diversification of economic base leads to a rise in literacy rates as it accentuates the need for literacy and provides fillip to rural literacy.

(viii) Another vital factor operating in favour of improving rural literacy is the phenomenal development of faster communication. Faster communication spells quicker travel of' new ideas, an accelerated process of modernization and a growing awareness among the people. This is bound to encourage the need for literacy and education and a competitive spirit among the people generating a dynamic outlook.

(ix) The trend towards globalization tends to reduce differentials between rural and urban areas. The rural areas with their traditional backwardness have greater potential for change and may even out do the urban areas in the process of change.

(x) The National Literacy Mission (NLM) launched in 1988 in pursuance of the National Policy on education, 1986 embarked on a vigorous programme of eradication of illiteracy through its Total Literacy campaign (TLC). By March 2003, it had already made 98 million people literate, 190 districts were in Total Literacy Campaign, 196 were in post literacy stage and 201 were in continuing education state stage. National Literacy Mission has devised three different stages of its literacy programme viz (i) the initial phase aiming at imparting functional literacy. (ii) Post literacy phase that consolidates and upgrades the programme to a self-reliant level. (iii) Continuing education phase comprising self-directed learning and its application through continuing learning. After the completion of the first two stages, the districts graduate to the continuing education stage. National Literacy mission hopes to bring the entire country to this level by the end of the 10th plan period i.e. 2007.

(xi) Sarva Shiksha Abhiyan, Is the national umbrella programme to universalize elementary education. The major objectives of this programme aim at sending all children to school of different kind by 2003, completing primary schooling by 2007 and completing 8 years of elementary schooling by 2010, India is committed to adopt strategies to equalize the gender and residential gap in elementary school education to all its children of 14 years by 2010.

(xii) Different states have evolved their own strategies to improve their female literacy. Rajasthan has involved the Panchayats to spearhead the campaign. Madhya Pradesh has its own Mahila Pradhan Bandhan andolan. The strategies of both Andhra Pradesh and Madhya Pradesh make case of Self-Help Groups as literacy centres. In Uttar Pradesh, network of 100 Non-Government Organizations has set up a programme aimed at making about 24 lakh women literate within a period of six months in eight low female literacy districts. Orissa has a similar programme in seven districts with less than 30 per cent female literacy. Bihar involves panchayat functionaries in the process along with women volunteer teachers and makes use of women's Self-Help Groups. The state hopes to cover about three million non-literate women in six to twelve months.

(xiii) A system of neoliterate societies has been introduced in some states. Increasing role of the community towards the programme, which is most desirable and even essential.

(xiv) The 86th constitutional amendment adding clause 21A to the right to life, in December 2002 guaranteed every child between the ages of 6-14 years, education up to the elementary stage as a fundamental right.

(xv) The United Nations General Assembly in its 56th session in 2001 adopted United Nations Literacy Decade (UNLD) towards achieving education for all (EFA). The United Nations Literacy Decade extended over 2003 – 2012 recognizes that literacy is essential for every child adult and youth of the 21st century.

Conclusion

Literacy is an important element of transformation and social economic and political development. India to-day is passing through its critical stage of demographic evolution. Here there are 933 women for every 1000 men, only 53.7% of women are literate as compared to 75.3% men, less than 10% of parliament seats, less than 15% cabinet positions, less than 4% of seats in High Courts and the Supreme Court, Less than 8% of administrators and Managers are represented by women—when women's enrolment in Universities/Colleges is currently 39.94 per cent, there are only 5 exclusive Women Universities and 1578 women colleges the country badly stands in need of an accelerated pace of literacy transition which alone can serve the cause of containing the menace of growing population which poses a serious danger to the progress of the country. A thrust of rural literacy assumes special significance in the context of India where more than 70 per cent of country's population lives in rural areas and the number of rural illiterates in the country is more than the total combined population of Japan, United Kingdom, Canada & Australia. As in rural areas more than two thirds of the population is still illiterate, urban rural literacy ratio still calls for more vigorous efforts specially among the rural female population"Rural women need to wake up and actively participate in the movement for universalisation of literacy. Special attention needs also to be paid to promote rural literacy among various special groups comprising Scheduled Castes, and Scheduled Tribes especially among the female components of these groups. Education the agent of basic changein the status of women and the source of empowerment demands the commitment and active involvement of all sections of the society. Those who have benefited from the education system have now the responsibility to ensure that others too get the opportunity to gain from it.

REFERENCES

Ashrit Radha R., (2006); *Health Status of Working Women,* Yojana, Director Publication Division, Ministry of Information and Broadcasting Soochana Bhawan. CGO Complex, Lodi Road, New Delhi- 110003, March, pp. 75-78.

Bhutani Smita and Vivek Nagpal, (2005); *Dynamics of Rural Literacy in India,* University News, Association of Indian Universities, AIU House, 16 Comrade Indrajit Gupta Marg, (Kotla Marg) New Delhi -110002, May 16-20, Vol 43, No. 20, pp. 5-16.

Khan Mohsin Ali, (2001); *Women's Education: Still a distant Dream,* Yojana, Director Publication Division, Ministry of I & B, Patiala House, New Delhi-110001, December, 2001, Vol. 45, pp. 40-43.

Sapru R.K. (Ed), (1989), *Women and Development,* Ashish Publishing House, 8/81 Punjabi Bagh, New Delhi- 110026, pp. 278-314.

Sarkar C.R., (2005); Women Literacy and India, University News, Association of Indian Universities, AIU House, 16 Comrade Indrajit Gupta Marg, (Kotla Marg), New Delhi -110002, July 18-24, Vol. 43, No. 29, pp. 7-10.

Sekhar Madhu R., (2001); *Girls Education: Opening the Window on to the World,* Yojana, Director Publication Division, Ministry of I & B, Patiala House, New Delhi-110001, November, Vol. 45, pp. 46-47.

Sharma Sheetal, (2006): *Educated Women, Empowered Women,* Yojana, Director Publication Division, Ministry of Information and Broadcasting Soochana Bhawan, CGO Complex, Lodi Road, New Delhi- 110003, October, Vol. 50, pp. 52-57.

Venkataiah S., (Ed.) (2001): *Women Education,* Anmol Publications, Pvt. Ltd., New Delhi 110002.

percent of country's population lives in rural areas and the number of rural illiterates in the country is more than the total combined population of Japan, United Kingdom, Canada & Australia. As a fact [illegible] more than two-thirds of the population is still illiterate [illegible] among the rural female population. Rural women need to wake up and actively participate in the movement for universalisation of literacy. Special attention needs also to be paid to promote rural literacy among various special groups comprising Scheduled Castes and Scheduled Tribes especially among the female components of these groups. Education, [illegible] the extent of basic [illegible] status of women and the source of empowerment [illegible] and active involvement of all sections of the society. [illegible] the education system [illegible] the responsibility to ensure that [illegible] the opportunity to get [illegible]

REFERENCES

[illegible] (2007) [illegible] Women, Yojana, [illegible] Publication Division, Ministry of Information and Broadcasting, [illegible] Bhawan, [illegible] Road, New Delhi [illegible] p. [illegible]

[illegible] (2002) [illegible] of Rural [illegible] Association of [illegible] Vol. [illegible] No. 23 [illegible]

[illegible] (2001) [illegible] Publication Division, Ministry of I & B, Patiala House, New Delhi, [illegible] December 2001, Vol. 45, pp. 40 [illegible]

[illegible] Women and [illegible]

[illegible] Association of Indian [illegible] New Delhi-110002, [illegible] Vol. 4 [illegible]

[illegible] (199[illegible]) [illegible] Yojana, [illegible] Publication Division, Ministry of I & B, Patiala House, New Delhi-110001, November, Vol. 45, pp. 45 [illegible]

[illegible] Yojana, Director, [illegible] Publication Division, Ministry of Information and Broadcasting, [illegible] Bhawan, [illegible] New Delhi [illegible] Vol. [illegible]

[illegible] New Delhi-110002.

WOMEN LITERACY FOR EMPOWERMENT

—TARULATA DEVI

"To awaken the people, it is women who must be awakened, Once she is in the move, the family moves, the village moves and the nation moves."

Jawaharlal Nehru

Introduction

Women constitute the most elegant resource of a society and is the dynamic source of power. They comprise the very backbone of a family with multiple role players of a mother, a wife, a pretty sister and a host of others. She is brought up in sheer neglect and utter discrimination. Their innocent childhood and rightful womanhood are sacrificed in the altar of family. A girl in her natal home is considered a temporary member and in her in laws home an outsider. A deep analysis of social, economic, political and educational panorama reveals the fact that in most developing countries in general and India in particular, the girl child is born into indifference and inferiority. There is persistent discrimination against the girl child which results in foeticide, infant mortality etc. Table 9.1 shows the declining gender ratio of India and Orissa respectively.

Declining Gender Ratio

Sex ratio has not only been unfavourable to women since the beginning of the century but has declined continuously as shown in the table India is among the eighteen countries of the world where the sex ratio is adverse to females. The 2001 census of India gives Indications like the sex ratio of 933 females for 1000 males in the population. Although the sex ratio in Orissa was more than 1000 from 1901 to I961 and in 2001 it is more than national ratio having 972 females for 1000 males.

Table 9.1 : Gender Ratio (1901-2001)

Census Year	*Sex ratio of 1000 Male India*	*Orissa*
1901	972	1037
1911	964	1056
1921	955	1086
1931	950	1067
1941	945	1053
1951	946	1022
1961	941	1001
1971	930	986
1981	934	981
1991	926	971
2001	933	972

Women Literacy

Litercy is the first step of empowerment of the individual; it opens the door to acquire knowledge . As literacy has significant bearing on every sphere of human activity, the extent of success in promoting literacy and reducing gender differences should be taken as indicator of women empowerment for effectively contributing to social development. An attempt is made to discuss the linkage between women's literacy and the search for equality and empowerment.

Female literacy is considered to be a more sensitive development as compared to overall literacy rates. Female iiteracy is negatively related with fertility rates, population growth rates, infant and child mortality rates and shows a positive association with female age at marriage, life expectancy participation in the modern sectors of the economy and above all with female enrolments.

Table 9.2 portrays the literacy rate of India for the last five

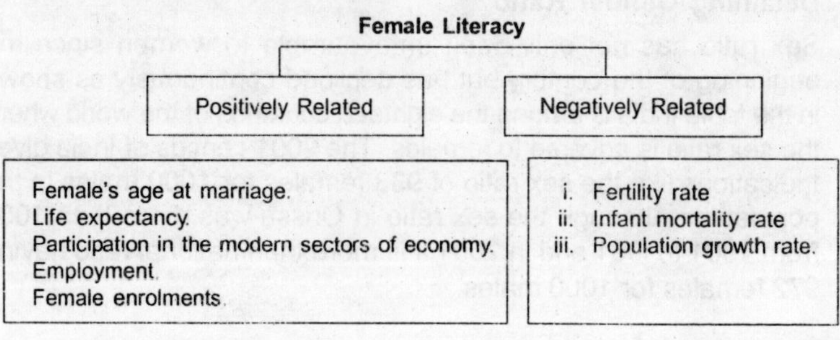

Table 9.2 : Literacy Rates in India (1951-2001)				
Census Year	*Persons*	*Males*	*Females*	*Male Female gap in literacy rate*
1951	18.33	27.16	8.86	18.30
1961	28.30	40.40	15.35	25.05
1971	34.45	45.96	21.97	23.99
1981	43.57	56.38	29.76	26.62
1991	52.21	64.13	39.29	24.84
2001	65.38	75.85	54.16	21.69

Source: Economic Survey, GOI, 2003-04.

decades which suggests that the comprehensive education policies of the goverment of India undertaken over the last few decades have been able to give a fill up to trigger the women's literacy rate in India. In the beginning of this century (1901) disparity in literacy rates for men (9.83%) and women (0.6%) was 9.23 which grew to 16.97% points in 1951 even after launching the planned developmental programme in 1951-52, this disparity has been perpetuated as is reflected in the male-female differences in literacy rates. The difference was as high as 26.62% points in 1981. The country has thus witnessed growing gender disparity in literacy. Obviously, even though literacy rate for women has gradually improved from less than 1% in 1901 to 54.16% in 2001, there has been a shortfall in efforts to bridge this gap. It is evident from the above data that after independence the overall literacy rate of India has been the highest during the decade 1991-2001. For the first time, the country witnessed a faster growth in female lIteracy that is 14.9% point (54.16%) in 2001 as against 39.29% in 1991 which is higher than the increase in the male literacy rate of 11.7% point (75.85%) in 2001 as against 64.13% in 1991. However the gender gap in literacy has eroded from 24.84% in 1991 to 21.69% in 2001. Regional disparities on the state of women's literacy are also pronounced. According to 2001 census among the states Kerala has the highest female literacy rate with (87.72%) where as Bihar recorded the lowest level of literacy. (33.12%).

In progressive states like Kerala the male-female literacy gap is minimum 6.34% and similar situation exists in Mizoram, Goa and Lakshadweep etc., where as this gap is higher in Bihar, Jharkhand and Chhatisgarh. This variation depicts the gap in social and over all human development among the states.

Table 9.3 : Literacy Rates in Orissa

Census Year	Persons	Males	Females	Male Female gap in literacy rate
1961	25.24	40.26	10.12	30.14
1971	26.18	38.29	13.92	24.37
1981	34.12	46.90	21.11	25.79
1991	48.55	62.37	39.42	22.95
2001	63.08	75.35	50.51	24.84

Table 9.4 : Rural Urban Literacy Rates of Females in Orissa.

Census year	Rural	Urban	Total Literacy
1951	4.87	22.33	7.93
1961	10.13	40.46	15.35
1971	15.52	48.84	21.97
1981	20.66	54.40	28.47
1991	30.62	64.05	39.29
2001	46.58	72.99	54.16

Source: Statistical Abstract of Orissa.

The 2001 census shows that the urban-rural female literacy gap was 27%. It needs special attention to reduce the gap. A glance at the literacy rate and enrolment in Orissa at various stages of education clearly reveals the sex disparities in education. Though the female literacy rate in the state increased from 4.5% in 1951 to 50.51% in 2001. It is still lower than the national average of 54.16% and also much lower than the male literacy rate of 75.35% in the state. However the gender gap in literacy rate of Orissa in 2001 (24.84) is more than the national average i.e. 21.69%. In rural areas the female literacy rate is 46.66% which is lower than the state average. It reflects that the socio-economic status of women in the state of Orissa is characterized by low female literacy, distressing health and nutritional deficiencies, low proportion of women employees in the organized sector and the declining proportion of the females in the total population. A striking feature is that, there is a wide variation between male and female literacy rate. Female literacy in rural areas is about half of the urban literacy. The literacy rate of rural female is 46.66%, and the urban female literacy is 72.87%. Besides the dropout cases of girls are very high in comparison to boys. Even today 60% of the female population in the country is illiterate with girls accounting for only 43.2% of the enrolment at the primary school stage and 39% at the upper primary stage.

- For development of femele education, educational institutions including Kanyashrams have been established exclusively for girls, particularly in low literacy tribal areas. Education for girls from primary to post-graduation level has been made free. Industrial and Technical Institutes and Polytechnic exclusively for women have been opened to provide them professional training.
- The Human Resource Development (HRD) Ministry's free education scheme for the single girl child is a welcome one. The Government should also take in to consideration the other factors responsible for illiteracy among female population. While the capacity to pay the fees is one of the factors there are other factors too like the security of the girls, accessibility of schools and the relevance of the curriculum that are also contributing illiteracy among female population.
- The scheme of condensed courses for education of adult women (2003-04) was started by the OSSWAB (Orissa State Social Welfare Advisory Board) with the objective of extending education and training to needy widows, destitute, desperate and economically backward women so as to enable them to acquire eligibility for suitable employment. Under the scheme, there is provision for conducting two years condensed course for primary [middle] H.S.C. examination passed and one year condensed course for H.S.C. failed candidates.
- The objective of the Balika Samridhi Yojana (BSY) (1997) scheme is to change the negative attitude of family as well as community towards girl child at birth and her mother, retention of girl's from primary to post-graduation level is free.
- National Programme of Education for Girls at Elementary Level (NPEGEL) are the programmes to motivate the girls to attened the schools with the support of community. This

has been launched in the year 2003-04 with the noble objective to provide additional support to education of girls at the elementary level.

- The Mahila Samakhya Scheme was introduced in the year 1989 for the education and empowerment of women in rural areas particularly from socially and economically marginalized group.
- Sarva Shiksha Abhiyan (SSA) is a comprehensive scheme seeks to bridge gender inequality by giving due emphasis to promote education of girl child in the society on a large scale and to afford them social justice, security and equity at par with the boy child.

Women Empowerment

The 20th century was an era of socio-cultural reforms, which sowed seeds for women's empowerment. The reformers constantly worked for bringing out attitudinal change in society especially towards women, who constitute 48% of total population in India. They strongly believed that empowerment of women was crucial for socio-economic and political progress of India. Even after 50 years of independence these women continue to live in a state of neglect and over exploitation. Scientific achievements and modernization are yet to make an impact on them. Given empowerment in terms of knowledge, information, the right environment and proper skills women can lead the nation to greater heights socially, economically and culturally. The concept of women empowerment was introduced at the International Women's Conference at Nairobi in 1985. The conference defined empowerment as a redistribution of social power and control of resources in favour of women. An important means of women's empowerment is economic independence through information, knowledge and necessary skills.

Education is a milestone for women empowerment because it enables them to respond to opportunities,to-challenge there traditional roles and change their lives. Education is one of the most important means of empowering women with the Knowledge, skills and self-confidence necessary to participate fully in the development process. Women are less represented in literacy sphere, employment in public and private sector, political sphere, administration, science and technology, self-employment etc. Teaching profession is considered more suitable for women.

The Government has adopted the policies and programmes for

the empowerment and upliftment of women as part of its various welfare measures. The Department of Women and Child Development (DWCD) has taken up various projects which are directed towards advancement of women. The National Policy for Empowerment of Women was adopted in the country in 2001 with the ultimate objective of ensuring women their rightful place in the society by empowering them as agents of socio-economic change and development.

Conclusion

The entire success of the family and nation depends on the women of the house and at the working place. The empowered new Indian woman should discover ways of blending religious commitment, cultural traditions and family obligations with new work styles and leadership in various areas. That envisages flowering of an individual, strengthening of community, building institution and strengthening our country.

Education helps a woman to earn an income in later life, participate actively in public life, determine her own fertility and achieve personal autonomy. The need of the hour is to empower women so that they can make the right choice in every sphere of life. They should be authorized to develop self-confidence, self-esteem, positive attitude and equity etc. The plan and programmes for women equality and empowerment through acceleration of educational advancement should be carried out with great vigour and sincerity and should be matched by strong administrative and financial support.

Women's education is a function of women's equality which will not come about by mere provision of rights but by the ability of women to use those rights. Let us conclude with the word of Shoma A. Chatterji that, "A woman can recognize her own worth, can identify the need to be an individual in her own right, and can assert herself in her own independent capacity only when she is educated. Education is the weapon she can use to fight the war of inequality between the illiterate and the educated. Education is the ticket that allows a woman to proceed on the journey towards economic independence and is the book that opens the pages of her civil rights to her."

REFERENCES

Chatterji, Shoma A., (1993), *The Indian Women in Perspective*. Ajanta Publications, New Delhi, p. 55.

Devendra, Kiran, (1994) *Changing Status of Women in India,* Vikas Publishing House Pvt. Ltd., New Delhi.

Govt. of India, (2003-2004), *Economic Survey,* p. 213.

Power, K.B. and Shafi, Zeenat, S., (Eds), (1999), *Women Participation in Higher Education,* AIU, New Delhi.

Sahoo, B., (Eds), (1990), *Women Employment in India,* Satanetra Publications, Bhubaneswar.

Sarkar, C.R., (2005), *Women Literacy and India,* University News, 43(29), AIU, New Delhi, pp. 7-10.

Srivastava Gouri, (2004), *Women's Empowerment : A Legacy and Commitment,* University News, 42(26), pp. 11-15.

Govt. of Orissa (2005), *Statistical Abstract of Orissa,* Directorate of Economics and Statistics, Orissa, Bhubaneswar.

10

WOMEN EDUCATION IN ORISSA—Trends and Challenges

—SUREKHA SUNDARI SWAIN

Introduction

One of the best ways to understand the spirit of a civilization and to appreciate its excellences and realize its limitations is to read position and status of women in it. (Altekar 1959). Women constituting about half of the total population of India, continued to remain insignificant for ages together. Women education received the least attention due to lack of clear concepts about aims and ideals of education. Education of women suffered from numerous setbacks, such as early marriage, poverty, gender discrimination, household chores etc. In spite of recommendations of the various committees and commissions the women education could not be developed up-to satisfaction and lagging behind.

Historical Prospective

Long before advent of the English people to power indigenous educational system was prevailing in Orissa both for boys and girls. There were three types of indigenous institutions such as Tols, Muktabs and Chatsalis. The tols were higher indigenous schools located normally in maths, holy places and big villages within Brahmin population with Sanskrit as the medium of instruction. The Muktabs were indigenous elementary schools for Muslims in Orissa teaching Persian & the Koran. The Chatsalis were village elementary schools as bases for the promotion of mass education.

In 1835 William Adam, a Christian Missionary conducted an educational enquiry in Bengal by order of Lord William Bentick the initiator of higher education in India. He mentioned the existence of 'Maths' (religious institutions of Hindus meant for charitable works) at Puri as the seats of various branches of Hindu learning. Oriya was the medium of instruction there. Oriya was also a medium in one hundred and eighty two schools even outside Orissa that was in Midnapore (Adam 1988). But education of girls in Orissa was domestic and was rarely formal or institutional. Attention to female education was marginal and its importance was not realized and accepted in the society.

Mrs. Smith started one Zenana Association in 1869 for the education of married girls. The Zenana (domestic teaching) started in April 1869 with six housewives only. By 1872, 126 women at their residence were educated. The Government and missionaries made joint efforts for the progress of women education. But the Hindu girls were not allowed to join those schools in fear of proselytism.

Abinash Chatterjee, a generous gentleman of Cuttack took great interest in the education of women. The Cuttack Hindu Girls' School started in his residence at Balu Bazar of Cuttack, with oniy six students. Financial assistance was given by the Government in 1873 and subsequently it turned in to a famous centre of women education in Orissa known as Ravenshaw Hindu Girls School. In order to increase enrolment of girls, free studentship was granted to the students. Inspite of this incentive very few Oriya girls were educated due to social customs and prejudices. General Report on Public Instruction, Bengal 1866-71, stated that among all the communities the Karanas (Class of Writers) were less conservatives since twelve Karan Girls were allowed to join the Bhubaneswar Boys School. During 1873-74 there were seven girls in the schools of Puri district and thirty nine in Cuttack district.

The policy of the Government was slightly revised as per the resolution of 13th Jan. 1876 so as to encourage the girls to attend mixed primary schools along with consideration of establishment of separate girls schools. J.A. Hopkins, Inspector of Schools recommended for establishment of separate primary schools for promotion of girls education in Orissa.

As the people had trust in indigenous schools, a reward of rupees six annually was given to the Abadhans (Teacher of Lower indigenous schools of the Hindus of Orissa) in order to increase the number of girls. This policy was first started at Puri in 1876-77, and there vvas amazing increase of the girls in those schools. The number of Brahmin girls was higher than those of other castes in the schools. The First Oriya book published for the girls, was

"Balikapath" by Kumar B. N. De of Balasore to attract girls towards education.

The Hunter Commission 1882-83 recommended for the appointment of women inspectresses and women teachers for the spread of women education. There were 33 special girls schools in Orissa, out of which 25 were in Balasore. six in Cuttack, and two in Puri. Out of these. 20 schools were managed by the Missionaries and rest were Hindu girls schools. The girls schools of Cuttack, Balasore and Bhadrak were considered best schools. Balasore was having greater facilities for women education due to the influence of Bengal. In 1889-90, Saraswati Bai, the first Oriya Girl passed the Middle English Scholarship examination from Cuttack town.

In Cuttack town there were two upper primary and five lower primary schools, besides Ravenshaw Hindu Girls School. In 1899. two Primary Schools at Chandini Chowk and Jholasahi were taken over by the Government and maintained by municipality. Five lower primary schools situated at Tulasipur. Buxi Bazar. Khatbinsahi. Mansinghpatna and Oriya Bazar were managed by the Missionaries. But till the end of 18th Century not a single high school or college was opened in Orissa for the education of Oriya girls.

The Simla Conference of 1901 recommended on the establishment of model primary schools, training schools and strengthening the staff of inspectresses. It stressed that Government should take more responsibility for the progress of female education. Steps were taken accordingly, but it could not achieve greater result.

In 1912, Bihar and Orissa were partitioned from Bengal and a new combined province of Bihar and Orissa was formed, as a result, the Oriya girls availed opportunities for educational improvement through various programmes and plans. 1913 was the pivotal year for the development of education for the Oriya girls when the Government took over the charge of Ravenshaw Hindu Girls school. Before the school was handed over to the Government, it was upgraded to a middle vernacular school in 1883. In 1901, there were 59 students in the school. Another girl school namely Cuttack Model Girls School was established at Cuttack in the year 1906 under the auspices of Mrs. Reba Roy, the niece of famous Oriya Poet Bhakta Kabi Madhusudan Rao only with seven students. In 1907, the enrolment increased to 45, and it received financial assistance from the Government. The first Muslim girl, the daughter of Nurul Huq took admission in that school in 1907, and set an example to the Muslim girls education (Utkal Dipika March 1907).

The eminent son of the soil of Orissa Mr. Madhusudan. Das. was the President of the new Managing Committee of the Ravenshaw Girls School. Miss. Shailabala Das, the adopted daughter of Madhusudan Das. after returning from London. took initiative for the improvement of the school and she became the secretary of the school. The school was converted to a Girls High School during 1908-09. In March 1913, the Government took over the charge of the school, and the ward 'Hindu' was excluded from the name of the school and it was known as Ravenshaw Girls High School. Mrs. A.E.Banks was appointed as first Principal of the school. (Education proceedings 1913). In 1917 the school was shifted from Kaligali to a building acquired by the Government near Gaurishankar Park at Cuttack.

In 1913, Mr. Hallaward, the Director sanctioned monthly cost of Rs. 35 for opening of a model school at Bhadrak. Appointment of female teacher, seclusion of primary schools, sanction of monthly stipend to all girls of primary schools were the measures to solve the problem of expansion of female education. A sum of Rs. 20866 was sanctioned to sister M. Claudio Secretary of Saint Joseph's Convent Girl's School at her request in 1914, (Bihar and Orissa Education Proceeding 1914).

The Government of Bihar and Orissa appointed the Female Education Committee by the resolution No. 1284 .E. dt. 8th June 1914 for the promotion of female education.

Development of College Education in Orissa

The Female Education Committee, 1914 recommended opening of intermediate classes in the girls' high schools at Cuttack and Bankipur of Bihar. If the enrolment increases to twenty then the establishment of a separate college would be considered, (Quinquennials Review 19 12-17)" and the Government accepted these recommendations.

Prior to this the Oriya girls were reluctant to go to Calcutta due to distance and lack of facilities for Oriya teaching there (Government of Bihar and Orissa. Education. Department 1915). The Government was providing scholarship of Rs. 10 for Intermediate of Arts and Rs. 20 for Bachelor of Arts girl students, who were studying in Bethune College at Calcutta. The only Onya girl Narmada Kar, the daughter of Bagmi Biswanath Kar was continuing her studies at Bethune college. The Utkal Sabha of June 23, 1912, requested the Government to increase her scholarship in order to enable her to continue B.A. there. But her case was refused by' the Government (Utkal Dipika 1915).

In 1912, a Board of Education was constituted when Bihar and Orissa were partitioned from Bengal, to study the problems of education of Mrs. Sailabala Das and Mrs. Banks represented Orissa. Through their initiative, the Government took steps to introduce Intermediate Arts classes in Ravenshaw Girls High School during the year 1915-16. Only three candidates attended I.A. classes, and the number increased to eight in 1916-17 and the number increased to thirteen in 1917-18. During 1919-20. the I.A. classes of this school was affiliated to the Patna University.

An Association of Women Teachers was formed under the chairmanship of the lady principal of Ravenshaw Girls' High School. In 1922-23, the intermediate classes in Ravenshaw Girls' High School were made permanent (Government of Bihar and Orissa. Education, 1924).

The Hartog Committee, 1929, accorded liberal support to females education. The Government laid down policy on 31st March 1930 for further expansion of women's education. In 1930, five women students took admission in Ravenshaw College, which was a mile stone in the movement of female education in Orissa to join a college meant for men. Thus, sixty two years after the establishment of Ravenshaw College, co-education had its beginning there in 1929-30.

In 1934, there were eight students in Intermediate classes of Ravenshaw Girls High School, of whom one was from Ranchi, one from Patna and another from Rajasthan. In 1936, steps were taken to appoint a qualified lady teacher from the Lady Irwing College of Delhi. The establishment of separate college for women was not felt necessary due to shortage of students.

Thus, with the efforts of the Missionaries, Government and eminent personalities of the soil, women education could be brought from the deep darkness to see the dawn of these days. The contribution of Madhusudan Das, the Pride of the state. Bhaktakabi Madhusudan Rao, Vyasakabi Fakir Mohan Senapati, Bagmi Biswanath Kar. Abinash Chatterjee, Sailabala Das and Reba Roy were remarkable. The liberal donations of the kings of Orissa could give a stand to the women's education. By 1936, only about sixty thousand Oriya Girls and women out of four million females in Orissa could come for education from elementary to college. There was no degree college meant exclusively for women in Orissa. There were 13 colleges in total in Orissa of which three were first grade colleges, six were second grade colleges, one training college. one medical college, and two oriental colleges. Law classes were attached to the Ravenshaw College, Cuttack.

The Establishment of Utkal University

Pandit Godabarish Mishra became the Education Minister, in 1941. who took active interest in establishment of the University. The Utkal University Act was passed by the Orissa Legislature on 30th June, 1943, and Utkal University came into existence from 2nd August 1943. William Hawthorne, I.C.S. was the first Chancellor and Mr. Pranakrushna Parija, I.E.S.. was the first Vice-Chancellor of the University. The University conducted its first examination in 1943-44. The new colleges of Manipur, Lakshyadives, Andaman, Nicobar and Sikkim were affiliated to Utkai University.

Establishment of Sambalpur and Berhampur University

In the year 1966, the Government of Orissa prepared a scheme of proposal for establishment of two universities at Sambalpur and Berhampur which was approved by Government of India & U.G.C. On first Jan 1967, the Sambalpur University was established and on 4th January it was formally inaugurated. Berhampur Uiiiversity was also established in the same year.

Trends

The post independence era of modern Orissa has spectacled giant growth in women education. The female literacy rate (aged 7 years and above) of Orissa has increased to 51% according to 2001 census as compared to 5% in 1951 (Fig. 10.1). However the levels of women literacy vary across the state from 21% in Malkangiri to 71% in Khurda (Fig. 10.2).

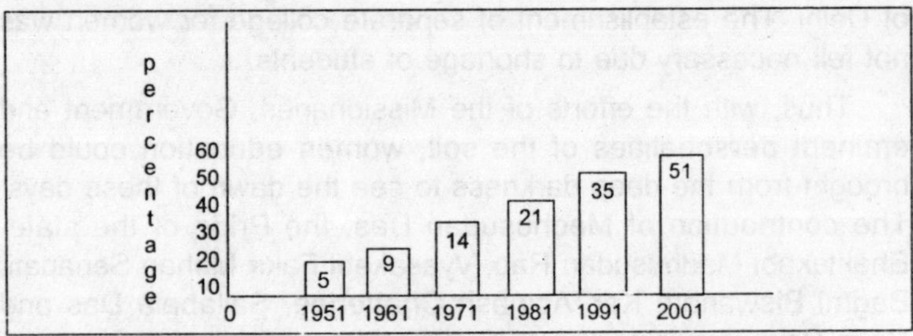

Fig. 10.1 : Female Literacy Rates of Orissa 1951-2001

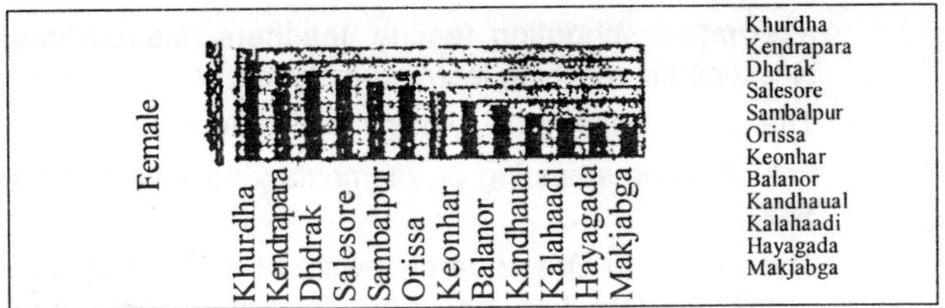

Fig. 10.2 : Female Literacy Rates Across Selected Districts of Orissa

However, between 1991-2001, female literacy went up by 16 percentage points the largest decadal increase ever. It so happens in the backward districts of Orissa. Further, the female literacy rate of India is 54% which is 3% higher than the female literacy rate of the State.

Challenges

In spite of upward trend in female literacy rate the status of women in Orissa has not developed to a satisfactory level. Despite the formation of National Human Rights Commission, State Human Rights Commission, Women Commission for Minorities and Commission for SC & ST and formation of a series of acts and legislations, the cases of violence against women is mounting at rapid rate. The most pernicious forms of violence are wife beating, domestic sexual harassment, dowry torture, dowry death, domestic cruelty, kidnapping, rape and murder, sex scandal, trafficking, acid attacks, bride burning, harassment at working place, daily humiliations and legal discriminations. Orissa ranks 25th in India in rape, dowry death and molestation cases, 19th in cruelty by husband or relatives and 21 in sexual harassment. Gender gaps in literacy is still prevailing (Census of India - 2001) between women and men of' Orissa. It is high in more educationally backward districts. The followings are some of the challenges faced by the people of the State irrespective of their sex, caste, community and culture.

- Around nine million women were identified as non-literates, which remains high with a total women population of around 18 million. Hence illiteracy begates illiteracy. (Census of India 2001).
- Lack of specialized and comprehensive data on learning achievement of girl children.
- Lack of infrastructure facilities in schools including

alternative schooling facility, teachers, classrooms, blackboards, teaching learning materials etc.

- The pupil teacher ratio remains low in the state.
- Fall of public spending on elementary education in the State.
- The women in Orissa hardly aware of or exercise their rights to education and equality, which the Indian Constitution provides.
- Women caught up in daily struggle for fuel, fodder and wage, have no time for anything else.
- Women well-defined social roles leave little room for education and critical thinking.
- Women are denied access to information and debarred of decision-making process. Even when they relate to Government schemes, they do so as passive recipient.
- Women are forced to read their environment with fear and suspicion.
- Conservative attitude, cultural value of the place and fear fro society and security which result in the poor women enrolment and withdrawal from educational institutions.
- Lack of moderate attitude of parents to enroll their daughters in the co-educational institutions.
- Demand for dowry discourages the parents to spend money on girl's education.
- Women Education is seen as a bad investment because a woman is treated as the property of others through marriage.

Strategies

Need-based and appropriate strategies may be developed to enhance girls' access to education, ensuring that content and process of education is sensitive to gender concerns and equal access assured for general, professional, technical and vocational education.

- A common core curriculum should be framed to promote a positive image of women. NCERT, SCERT, Board, Council and Universities should intensify activities by developing gender sensitive curriculum, removing sense bias from textbooks, training of the trainees and teachers.

- The Government, non-Government agencies, civil societies, political parties, religious leaders, teachers, people, representatives, community and media must come forward to generate conducive atmosphere for the education of the women and reshaping their mindset.
- Department of Education and other departments connected with education should prepare a concrete action plan addressing gender related concerns in their specific area of work.
- At the national and the state level documentation and monitoring unit should be created to ensure gender issues into policies, programmes and scheme.
- Need-based and local specific studies may be taken up-to identify the existing bias and deficiencies and suggest remedies and modalities to do away with these.
- The services of electronic, print and traditional media should be utilized to create equal opportunities for women and girls playing a complementary and supportive role in awareness generation, dissemination of information and, communication.
- Foundation courses should be designed and introduced at different stages of education with a view to promote empowerment of women.
- National and International resources must be reallocated in favour of girls' education.
- To widen access to vocational, technical, professional education at all levels breaking gender stereotypes.
- To gear up formal, non-formal, alternative education, bridge course, open school, distance education mode and literacy campaigns to accelerate progress and to reach the unreach.
- To increase the incentives and facilities for girls' education.
- To increase the no. of female educational administrators and managers.

REFERENCES

Altekar, A.S., (1959), *Position of women in Hindu Civilization.* Delhi Motilal Banarasi Das.

Govt. of India, (1986, 1992), *National Policy on Education*, Ministry of Human Resources, Department of Education, New Delhi.

UNICEF, (1992), *Strategies to Promote Girls' Education Policies and Programmes that Work*.

UNESCO, (1996), *Learning the Treasure Within*, Report of the International Commission on education for the Twenty-First Century.

11

WOMEN EDUCATION —A Challenging Issue

—SANJAY KETAN SWAIN

Women's Education need special Focuss in the context of globalisation. It has been rightly mentioned by Gandhiji, "If you educate a boy, you educate only one individual but if you educate a girl; your educate the whole family." Hence, importance of education of women has been recognised since the achievement of independence. The contribution of Indian women has been credible to the country's development process since independence. It has been a source of unique strength for reaching national goals.

As human beings, it is recognised that male and female are equal in status and in other social aspects of life Since, time immemorial, the women have been provided with priority of status and right in the society. Perhaps no data in the history of modern India is of greater importance in the emancipation and education of the Indian women than the data of our freedom.

Women's rights have been strengthened from time to time since independence. The constitution of India accords utmost importance to the welfare and development of children and women. So there is a constitutional obligation to provide special focus to girls education in view of constitutional provisions and various articles. The constitution has an impressive list of provisions for children as it not only grants equality and prohibits discriminations of caste, sex and creed, but also protects childhood from exploitation and abuse. Hence there is a need to :

- eliminate all forms of discrimination against the girl child,
- safeguard the rights of girl child,

- protect the girl child from the economic exploitation,
- protect the girl child health,
- eliminate the negative cultural attitudes.

Education for girls from legal point of view have also been visualised. Many laws are also enshrined in the constitution to protect the rights of girls. Women's rights have been strengthened from time to time. The different enactments like the Special Marriage Act, 1954, Hindu Marriage Act, 1955, Hindu Succession Act, 1956 and Hindu Adoption and the Maintenance Act, 1956 were principally responsible for this, particularly in respect of Hindu Women. Therefore, providing education to women is a necessity.

If we look into the cultural context, we see girls are distinguished from boys in terms of their .roles and responsibilities. But in modern context both need to grow economically and play multidimensional roles for successful life in every day situations.

There is a widespread feeling that girls need special attention in terms of providing educational opportunities. Democracy cannot flourish politically without the education of girls. Further, Universalisation of Elementary Education is possible when all the girls are educated alongwith boys. As it is a constitutional obligation, a sincere effort is necessary in order to achieve this objective.

Education improves health and hygiene, diet and living conditions of women. There is a relationship between educational levels of the women and mortality rates. Higher the education, lower the mortality rate. Inthis context, all the commissions including the Kothari Commission stressed on the need for providing impetus to girls' education.

In recent years it has become increasingly evident that women are lagging behind a great deal both in availing of the benefits of development and as participant in the process of development due to several socio-economic-cultural-political impediments. This has become a cause for concern, since women constitute a number of several millions and nearly half of our population. Women receive only a small share of developmental opportunities. So they are at the cross-roads. Undoubtedly, India faces an uphill task in the field of population explosion, mounting poverty, increasing illiteracy and women welfare etc. Education is one of the vital sectors which needs to be co-ordinated with women welfare sector.

Keeping in view the above scenario some of the drawbacks of

girls' education in a formal system may be mentioned here. The drawbacks are :

- Inadequacies in teaching - learning environment.
- Lack of adequately oriented, motivated or committed teachers.
- Lack of feeling of owning the school by the community.
- Lack of integrated, co-ordinated effort between different government and non-government agencies.
- Lack of adequate and properly equipped special schools to cater to the needs of girl children with special needs.

It is realised that the formal system of education will not be able to reach all children of the country particularly girls, whose participation in the school system is hindered by social and economic conditions. Therefore, the National Policy on Education 1986 provided for a systematic and large scale flexible programme for non-formal education to enable the children to learn at their own place and environment about the education of comparable quality. The concept behind the system is that if the child cannot go to the school, the school shall go to the child. In due course, many social and economic programmes like non-formal education for girls, Integrated Rural Development Programme were evolved exclusively for women. The benefit derived from these programmes had to be substained and this was posing a challenge.

Girls' education is free throughout the country upto Class - XII. In some states, it is free even at college level. Removing gender in-equalities in enrolment and eliminating gender bias in curriculum has been a priority area in the National Policy on Education as updated in 1992. The District Primary Education Project (DPEP) lays special emphasis on female literary, 60% of the total learners in the National Literacy Mission are women, 50% of the teachers recruited under the scheme of Operation Blackboard will be women. Another scheme called 'Mahila Samakhya' (Improvement of women) has also created a new awareness among women and generated demand for education.

Some of the factors which motivate the girls' education may be as follows :

- Parents motivational compaigns.
- Facilities and incentives.

- Mother Associations.
- Community awareness programmes.
- Quality enrichment programmes.

Today, the educational scene in independent India is completely transformed. India is one of the largest educational systems of the world with largest number of primary schools and the largest number of graduates from Indian Universities. In brief, the progress made by India in the field of women's education till date is unprecedented. Its greatest achievement is that it has made the best endeavours to establish a National System of Education on which the importance of women education has been emphasised more significantly.

The education of women is an integral part of National development. The education of girls, therefore, should be emphasised not only on grounds of social justice, but also because it accelerates social transformation. There is still a dearth of systematic planning for women upliftment which pose a great challenge before the country.

12

DEVELOPMENT IN THE HIGHER EDUCATION OF WOMEN IN INDIA

—Bimal Charan Swain

Women constitute the most elegant resource of a society. They comprise the very backbone of a family with multiple role players of a mother, a wife, a sister and a host of others. Education is considered as an important instrument in improving the status of women and consequently there have been efforts to improve the access of girls and women to education in India and abroad.

The United Nations General Assembly declared the International Year of Women in 1975 followed by the International Women's Decade and organized three World Conferences in 1975 at Mexico, at Copenhagen in 1980 and at Nairobi in 1985. The Fourth World Conference Beijing in 1995 emphasized that gender equality must be recognised as an issue of universal concern benefitting all. The World Summit held during November 25-28, 1996 at Trinidad and Tobago was the first conference of Ministers responsible for women affairs. The World Education Forum (26-28 April, 2000) made a commitment of achieving 50 per cent improvement in levels of adult literacy by 2015, especially for women and an equitable access to basic and continuing education for all adults.

Development of women has been receiving the attention of the Government of India right from the very First Plan (1951-56). 'Empowerment of Women' became one of the nine primary objectives in the Ninth Plan (1997-2002). In the Tenth Plan (2002-2007) emphasis was given on social and economic empowerment of women and gender justice.

Policies and Programmes on Education and Empowerment of Women in India

Serious efforts were made in India after independence to encourage the education of women. A National Committee on Women's Education chaired by Mrs. Durgabai Deshmukh was set up in 1956 to examine comprehensively the problems of women's education and a "Council of Women's Education" was set up in 1956. Hansa Mehta Committee (1961) and Bhaktvatsalam Committee (1965) were also appointed to look into the problems, specifically of curriculum for girls and lack of public support for girls education. All the committees and commissions appointed by Government of India after independence have given importance to women education.

National Policy on Education (1986) on Women Education

Regarding education of women the National Policy on Education (1986) emphasises that :

> *Education will be used as an agent of basic change in the status of woman. In order to neutralise the accumulated distortions of the past, there will be a well-conceived edge in favour of women. The National Education System will play a positive, interventionist role in the empowerment of women. It will foster the development of new values through redesigned curricula, textbooks, the training and orientation of teachers, decision makers and administrators, and the active involvement of educational institutions. This will be an act of faith and social engineering. Women's studies will be promoted as a part of various courses and educational institutions encouraged to take up active programmes to further women's development.*

Programme of Action of Revised National Policy on Education (NPE) (1992) and its Role for Women Education

The Programme of Action of Revised NPE (1992) recommended that the following measures will be taken to make education an effecfive tool for women's empowerment.

- Enhance self-esteem and self-confidence of women;
- Building a positive image of women by recognizing their contribution to the society, polity and the economy;
- Developing ability to think critically;
- Fostering decision making and action through collective process;
- Enable women to make informed choices in areas like

education, employment and health (especially reproductive health);

- Ensuring equal participation in developmental processes;
- Providing information, knowledge and skill for economic independence;
- Enhancing access to legal literacy and information relating to their rights and entitlements in society with a view to enhance their participation on equal footing in all areas.

The National Policy for Empowerment of Women (2001) through Education

Government of India has enacted the National Policy for the Empowerment of Women : 2001. The goal of the policy is to bring about an advancement, development and empowerment of women. Regarding education of girls and women the policy portrays that :

> *Equal access to education for women and girls will be ensured. Special measures will be taken to eliminate discrimination, universalize education, eradicate illiteracy, create a gender sensitive educational system, increase enrolment and retension rate of girls and improve the quality of education to facilitate life long learning as well as development of vocational/ technical skills by women. Reducing the gender gap in secondary and higher education would be a focus area. Sectoral time targets in existing policies will be achieved, with a special focus on girls and women, particularly those belonging to weaker sections including the Scheduled Castes/ Scheduled Tribes/Other Backward Classes/ Minorities. Gender sensitive curricula would be developed at all levels of educational system in order to address sex stereotyping as one of the causes of gender discrimination.*

Higher Education for Women in India

India is the second largest populated country in the world. Women constitute 48.2 per cent of total population in India. The first three universities established in the country in 1857 at Kolkata, Chennai and Mumbai. It was only in 1877 that Calcutta University opened its door for girls. The efforts made by Indian Education Commission (1882-83) led to a beginning of women participation in higher education. Incentive for women education also came through Government Resolution on Education Policy (1913). The First Women's College was opened at Lucknow in 1901. In

Mumbai, Wilson College was the first to admit women in 1886. In 1916, the first Women's University i.e. S.N.D.T. Women's University was established in Mumbai.

At the time of independence in 1947, there were only 20 universities and 500 colleges in the country. During 2002-2003, there were 300 universities including 81 deemed to be universities. There are five women's universities in India. They are S.N.D.T. Women's University, Mumbai, Mother Teresa Women's University, Kodai Kanal, Banasthali Vidya Peeth, Banasthali, Rajasthan, Avinasilingam Institute of Home Science and Higher Education for Women, Coimbatore and Shri Padmawathi Mahila Vishwavidyalaya, Tirupati.

The past decades have witnessed a great increase in the number of women's colleges which has been presented in Table 12.1.

Table 12.1 : Number of Women Colleges in India

Year	*Number of Women Colleges*
1993-1994	1033
1994-1995	1107
1995-1996	1146
1996-1997	1195
1197-1998	1260
1998-1999	1359
1999-2000	1503
2000-2001	1578
2001-2002	1625
2002-2003	1650*

* Provisional

Source : UGC Annual Report 2002-03.

There were 1033 women colleges in India in 1993-94 which increased to 1260 in 1997-98, 1503 in 1999-2000 and 1650 in 2002-03. There were 33 women's studies and development centres and six women's cells supported by the UGC. Women's studies have been attributed as a social need in order to develop women academically and make them capable to face all problems. Women Studies Centres have organized a total of 29 UGC refresher courses in the subject from 1997-98 to 2003-2004.

Enrolment of Women in Higher Education in India

The percentage of women's enrolment in higher education in India from 1950-51 to 2000-2001 has been presented in Table 12.2.

Table 12.2 : Percentage of Women in the Total Enrolment at Higher Education Level

Year	*Higher Education (Degree and above)*
1950-51	10.0
1955-56	14.6
1960-61	16.0
1965-66	20.4
1970-71	20.0
1975-76	23.2
1980-81	26.7
1985-86	33.0
1990-91	33.3
1991-92	32.3
1993-94	33.5
1994-95	34.0
1995-96	37.2
1996-97	38.2
1997-98	34.8
1998-99	38.8
1999-2000	39.9
2000-2001	36.9

Source : Selected Educational Statistics - 2000-2001.

Table 12.2 reveals that the participation of women in higher education has increased from 10 per cent in 1950-51 to 36.9 per cent in 2000-2001. Distribution of women enrolment by States and Union Territories (2001-02) show that Kerala with 60 per cent topped in terms of women enrolment as a percentage of total enrolment, followed by Goa 58.6 per cent, Andaman and Nicobar Islands 57.8 per cent, Chandigarh 55.5 per cent, Punjab 52.9 percent and Pondicherry 52.6 per cent. Bihar records the lowest women enrolment of 23.0 per cent in higher education.

The distribution of women enrolment faculty wise in India has been presented in Table 12.3.

Table 12.3 : Women Enrolment by Faculty (2002-03)

S. No.	*Faculty*	*Women Enrolment*	*Percentage of total women enrolment*
1.	Arts	18,89,799	51.13
2.	Science	7,36,890	19.94
3.	Commerce/Management	6,08,949	16.48
4.	Education	67,096	1.81
5.	Engineering/Technology	1,54,041	4.17
6.	Medicine	1,34,364	3.63
7.	Agriculture	9,332	0.25
8.	Veterinary Science	2,982	0.08
9.	Law	61.947	1.68
10.	Others	30,564	0.83
	Total	26,95,964	100.00

Table 12.3 shows that enrolment of women in the faculty of Arts has been 51.13 per cent of the total enrolment, followed by the faculty of Science (19.94 per cent), faculty of Commerce (16.48 per cent), Engineering and Technology (4.1 7 per cent), Medicine (3.63 per cent) and Education (1.81 per cent). It is lowest in Veterinary Science i.e. (0.08 per cent).

Women in Administrative Positions in Higher Education

The number of women administrators along with their position in Indian Universities has been presented in Table 12.4.

Table 12.4 : Women Administrators and Their Position in Indian Universities

Administrative Position	*Number*
Vice-Chancellors	12
Pro-Vice Chancellors	3
Registrars	7
Deans	72
Directors	13
Librarians	12

Source: AIU Handbook of Indian Universities, 2000.

Table 12.4 shows that the representation of women in higher education at the administrative position is low. But, it indicates that women are accessible to the leadership positions in higher education.

Suggestions

Participation of women in higher education in India has been improving and considerable progress has been made. A lot needs to be done. The following suggestions may be taken in to consideration to raise the access of women to higher education in India.

- Efforts must be made to retain the girls/women in primary and secondary levels and to reduce dropout rate at these levels.
- In planning for modernization the women employment efforts should be taken into account.
- Impressive achievements and innovative approaches and efforts of both government and non-governmental agencies have led to progress in education in terms of access, enrolment, retention and quality in women education. Women colleges have to be part of such activities.
- The educational institutions will have to organise training camps for personality development and encourage girls and women to participate and take up leadership roles.
- Seats need to be increased for women in technical disciplines like law, medicine, engineering, veterinary science etc.
- Women colleges need to be established in different areas of the country.
- Hostel facilities for women students need to be expanded at different levels.
- Stipends and fellowships may be made available to women at higher education level to take up research in different areas.
- For the higher education the women of SC and ST community, need to be empowered. To bring awareness among them regarding the importance of higher education, non-formal and adult education centres should be opened in every village.

- Vocational courses such as nurshing. fashion design. hotel management and computer application should be introduced in colleges to suit the needs of the women.
- Women's studies centres are to be strengthened for undertaking relevant research, training, extension, curriculum development, developing teaching materials, documentation, publication etc.

REFERENCES

Goel, M., (1998), "Women in Science and Technology in India", *University News,* Vol. 36, No. 6.

Government of India, (1986), *National Policy on Education (1986).* Ministry of Human Resource Development, New Delhi.

Government of India, (1992), *Nationl Policy on Education - Programme of Action (1992),* Ministry of Human Resource Development, New Delhi.

Saxena, S. (1996), "Higher Education for Women - A Case Study of Vikram University, Ujjain", *University News,* January 22.

Srivastava, N., (2005), "Empowerment of Women Through Higher Education", *University News,* Vol. 43, No. 47.

Swain, B.C., (2005), "Women Education in India After Independence, *Paper* Presented in the National Seminar, S.B. Women's College, Cuttack, 15-16 January 2005.

Swain, B.C., (2006), "Empowering Women in India The Educational Dimension", *Souvenir,* UGC Sponsored National Seminar on "Empowering Women in India", Ravenshaw College, Cuttack 27-28 October, 2006.

Swain, B.C. and Das. R., (2006), "Women Education in Orissa", *Souvenir,* UGC Sponsored Seminar on "Women Education in KBK District" of Orissa, Government Women's College, Bhawanipatna, 29th and 30th March, 2006.

13

WOMEN EDUCATION —Issues and Rethinking

—RABINARAYAN SAHOO

Introduction

The Manusmruti says, "Where women are respected, there the Gods delight and where they are not there all work and efforts come to naught. There is no hope of rise for that family or country where they live in sadness."

It is only through the education of women, that we can expect better atmosphere at homes, better hygienic condition, greater production, greater reduction in fertility rate so essential for our economic prosperity and happier family life. Therefore, late Pandit Jawaharlal Nehru rightly stressed that education of boy is education of one person, but education of girl is the education of the entire family.

Women, who are about the half of the total population, receive a meager share of developmental opportunities. Much is discussed in various committees, commissions and conferences on equality, development and empowerment of women. But reality is far from speculative truth. Women do not have equitable access to literacy, education, food, nutrition, health, employment or in political and economic decision-making process.

Realising the importance of women's equality NPE 1986 has stressed that "Education will be used as an agent of basic change in the status of woman. The National Education system will play a positive, interventionist role in the empowerment of Women".

Status of Women In India

Women in India are very backward socially, economically and politically. The only way to bring normalcy in this field is educating all the women and providing facilities at an accelerated pace.

Gandhiji observed in "True Education", "The question of the education of children cannot be solved unless efforts are made simultaneously to solve the women's education."

Dr. Radhakrishnan has very emphatically stated, "Women are human beings and have as much right to full development as men have. The position of women in any society is a true index of its cultural and spiritual level." Indian Education Commission wrote, "In the struggle for freedom, Indian women fought side by side with men. This equal opportunity will have to continue in the fight against hunger, poverty, ignorance and ill-health."

Social Status

Our Women are still shackled to traditions, customs, age-old superstitions and believes, orthodoxy, dogmatism and conservatism still prevail. There is no awareness and consciousness among women so that they can take up their rights and responsibilities. They remain suppressed by their husbands, spend most of their time in kitchen work, remain economically dependant throughout life and are viewed as inferior in the men-dominated society.

Political Status

Parliament has enacted laws giving equal status and rights to women in marriage, divorce, inheritance etc. Articles 14,15 and 16 of the Indian constitution guarantee absence of discrimination on the ground of sex etc. Women have got full right of franchise like men, as per Directive principles of state policy. In spite of various constitutional provisions women are not getting out of the old shackles and prison walk of life. However, in the past women had made a good contribution to the national struggle since then, they have been leading the country in the social and political fields.

Economic Status

Women are generally economically dependant and backward. They are not economic contributors. Some women are working in agriculture, factories and labour colonies and are taking up unskilled jobs. Out of the total labour force of women nearly 75% work as agricultural labourers, 15% in industries and 10% (educated women) in various institutions. There is a great dearth of women scientists, doctors, engineers and teachers and social workers for rural and backward areas.

Health Status

On the average women tend to live longer than men. But in certain African and Asian countries, the discrimination of women through neglect of their health and nutrition is such that they have shorter life expectancy. It is not an aberration that while women often grow and prepare the food for the entire family, women in most countries including India continue to be fed least and also fed last. Men and children feed first, the quality and nutritious food and what ever remains then, they eat. One of the greatest health risks for women in developing and underdeveloped countries is child birth. Maternal mortality rate in these countries are more than 15 times higher than in the developed countries. In India due to dowry practice, girl children are not allowed see the light through illegal and forceful abortion.

Employment Status

In developing countries, women have few job opportunities than men. Women are crowded into low-skilled and low-status jobs due to lack of access to education and information. In the industrial sphere, women are mostly engaged in the house-hold industries which offer uncertain and low-paid seasonal job. Due to engagement at home, child rearing, lack of support facilities like creches, women are forced to work part-time or on temporary basis. In most countries, employed women get less than men for same kind of physical. work. Wage discrimination is a common phenomenon in almost all countries of world.

Administrative Status

The participation of women in top level administration in appreciable numbers at the level of decision-making and enforcement in India is comparatively very low with the total number of women employed at all levels in various ministries. Moreover, there seems to be a practice of gender stereotyping women in the allocation of functions. It is observed women administrators are invariably given charge to subjects like social welfare, health, education, women and child development, rehabilitation, sports, youth welfare and the like.

Present Status

The United Nations Declaration on the elimination of the discrimination against women (1967) took note of the great contribution made by women to social, political, economic and cultural life and the part they play in the family and particularly in the rearing of children and recommended the following Article 9 of the declaration "all appropriate measures shall be taken to ensure to girls and women, married or unmarried, equal rights with men in education at all levels."

In the sphere of higher education professional courses and Universities, number of women teachers are also not encouraging although teaching profession is considered more suitable for women. In the corporate sector, women participation is also very small.

A deep analysis of social, economic, political and educational panorama reveals the fact that most developing countries in general and India in particular the girl child is born into indifference and inferiority. She is caught in the web of cultural deprivation, social prejudices that influence her individual growth and moulds her into a submissive and self-sacrificing entity whether she is a daughter, wife, mother or sister. She is brought up in sheer neglect and utter discrimination.

The need of the hour is to empower women so that they can make right choice in every sphere of life. Women can be made more aware of the need to control families by resorting to literacy drives and educative campaigns. Besides, it is also equally important to endow them with the power to execute their will—the will to withstand, social and family pressure and to assert their right to arrest the growth of family-size.

Women Education, Its Major Issues

From time to time the following committees and commissions have expressed concern regarding slow progress of girls and women education in India. Reference may be made to the following in this regard :

- The University Education Commission 1948-49.
- Smt. Durgbati Dashmukh Committee 1959.
- Smt. Hansa Mehta Committee 1962
- M. Bhaktavalsalam Committee to look into the causes of support particularly in rural areas for girls education and to enlist public co-operation.
- Indian Education Commission 1964-66.
- National Policy on Education 1968.
- Report of the Committee on the status of women in India 1974.

- Challenge of Education 1985.
- National Policy on Education 1986.

The causes of slow progress of women education as envisaged by the above committees and commissions are :

- Economic backwardness of the rural community.
- Lack of proper social attitudes in the rural areas for the education of girls.
- Lack of educational facilities in rural areas.
- Lack of women teachers.
- Lack of proper guidance and supervision.
- Lack of proper incentives to parents and children.
- Lack of suitable curriculum.
- Co-educational aspects.

Steps for the Amelioration of Women Education

Role of National Committee on Women Education

A National Committee on women education was constituted for reviewing the progress of women's education in the country and suggested measures for further development and improvement. The main recommendations of the committee are :

- Priority should be given to women education in the further programme of the development of education in the country.
- Discrimination between the education of boys and girls should be curbed and both should expand on an equal footing.
- The National Government should encourage States to launch various programmes associated with the development of women's education.
- Proper facilities and protection should be provided to women teachers serving in rural areas.

Other Suggestive Measures

- Free uniforms and free books to the needy and deserving children should be provided.
- Attendance scholarships which serve as a compensation to the parents should be given. This will ensure reduction of wastage and stagnation.
- Mid - day meals should be made available free of charge.

- Separate schools for girls at the middle and high school stages should be established where needed.
- School mothers in co-education primary schools should be appointed.
- Creches and nursery classes wherever possible should be opened.
- Public opinion in favour of girls' education should be created.
- Hostel for girls at the middle and high school stages should be provided.
- Maintenance stipends to girls residing in hostels for meeting their boarding and lodging expenses, at least in part should be provided.
- Subsidised transport facilities, wherever necessary and possible should be given.
- All priorities to be given to the construction of suitable buildings for girls' schools.
- Free education for girls up to the school leaving certificate examination must be made available.
- A large number of training institutions has to be provided for women, especially in the backward states. These institutions should generally be located in rural areas and they should generally recruit their trainees from that area.

Role of Task Force on Women and Violence

As per the recommendations of the workshop held in 1994 on violence against women in Orissa organized by Oxfam a NGO "Task Force on Women and Violence" was set up on 23rd December, 1999 with the following objectives.

- Support to victims of Gender Violence.
- Legal Reforms.
- Law Enforcement.
- Media Management.
- Public Education.

However, the task force on women and violence is working for the cause of women education in our State.

- It facilitates public education programmes for creating awareness of laws relating to women's rights in collaboration with the Police Department.

- Campaign on issues related to atrocities on women and highlight slags in action in case of gender violence by authorities.
- Discuss and debate on prominent and pertinent social issues bringing together in one platform various stakeholders.
- Conduct training programme, workshops on women education, violence, legal interventions etc. for different groups in the Society.

Conclusion

Women education should be given due importance in the present day society. While we are rededicating ourselves for the cause of women empowerment we must believe in the words of Robert Frost.

The woods are lovely, dark and deep,
But I have promises to keep,
And miles to go before I sleep,
And miles to go before I sleep.

Then only the development of society in general and women in particular will be possible.

14

SOME STRATEGIC EFFORTS TOWARDS THE EDUCATION OF WOMEN IN INDIA

—Rajalakshmi Das

Introduction

The status of a nation can very well be assessed by judging the status of women. Women who number 498.7 million according to 2001 census, represent 48.2 per cent of India's population of 1,027.01 million. Women of India have been affected more by poverty, lack of opportunities and facilities owing to the innate discrimination prevalent in our society. They do not have an equal status with men. Despite many international conventions affirming women's rights, girls and women are still more victims of domestic as well as social violence. Practically women's education is the antecedent to women's empowerment—the need of the hour around the globe.

The 20th century really marks the beginning of the process of educating, developing and empowering women. There has been a global effort with a strong support from the United Nations to understand the discrimination and restore a status to women.

Rationale for Women Education

Regarding education of women the University Education Commission (1948-49) remarked that "there can not be an educated people without education of women. If general education has to be limited to men or to women, the opportunity should be given to women, from them it would definitely be passed to the next generation". Education Commission (1964-66) also emphasised,- "For full development of human resources, the improvement of human beings and for moulding the character of children during the most impressionable period of infancy, the education of women is of great importance than that of men".

Education has been considered as an important instrument in improving the status of women and consequently there has been efforts to improve the access of girls and women to education. According to 2001 Census literacy rate of India is 65.38 per cent. Gender based literacy status indicates that 75.85 per cent of males and 54.16 per cent of females are literate in our country. Female literacy rate has improved from 8.66 per cent in 1951 to 54.16 per cent in 2001. There is a gap between the literacy rates of boys and girls at the school stage. Inspite of several interventions including the latest National Programme on Education for Girls at Elementary Level (NPEGEL) the progress is not satisfactory. Education of girl child needs special focus in the context of achieving Universalisation of Elementary Education. There is a constitutional obligation to provide special focus to girls' education. Article 14 of the constitution emphasises equal rights and opportunities to men and women. Article 15 prohibits discrimination on any ground and renounce the practices derogatory to women. Article 23 states "Traffic in human beings and beggary and other similar forms of forced labour are prohibited" and ... Article 24 states "No child below the age of 14 years shall be employed to work ... in any other hazardous employment". Article 42 states. "Provisions for just and human conditions of work and maternity relief". Article 45 emphasises. "Free and compulsory education for all children until they complete the age of 14 years". Article 47 emphasises. "Raising the level of nutrition and the standard of living of its people" and Article 73 and 74 emphasise. "Participation of women in the political and grassroot development process" .93rd Constitutional Amendment recognizes "Elementary Education as Fundamental Rights of children." There is a widespread feeling that girls need special attention in terms of provision of educational opportunities.

Government Policies on Women Education in India

After independence, steps have been taken to provide more educational opportunities to women. Several commissions and committees have been constituted to implement the educational programmes and monitor their progress. Some landmarks on women education are the recommendations of National Committee on Women's Education (1958-59), Committee on Differentiation of Curricula for Boys and Girls (1961), Committee to look into the causes of lack of public support particularly in rural areas for Girls' Education and enlist Public Co-operation (1963). Committee on the Status of Women (1971-74), Five Year Plans (First Five Year Plan 1951- 56) to Tenth Five Year Plan (2002-07), National Policy on Education (1986), Programme of Action (1992), National Commission on Self-employed Women and Women in the informal Sector (1987-88), National Prospective Plan for Women's Education (1988-2000 A.D.), National Policy for the Empowerment of Women (2001) and National Curriculum Framework of NCERT (2005).

National Policy on Education (1986) on Women Education

The National Policy on Education (1986) emphasises that Education will be used as an agent of basic change in the status of woman. In order to neutralise the accumulated distortions of the past there will be a well-conceived edge in favour of women. The National Education System will play a positive interventionist role in the empowerment of women. It will foster the development of new values through redesigned curricula, textbooks, the training and orientation of teachers, decision makers and administrators, and the active involvement of educational institutions. This will be an act of faith and social engineering. Women's studies will be promoted as a part of various courses and educational institutions which may take up active programmes to further women's development.

The Programme of Action of Revised NPE (1992) on Women Education

The, Programme of Action of Revised National Policy on Education (1992) recommended that the following measures will be taken to make education an effective tool for women's empowerment.

- Enhance self-esteem and self-confidence of women.
- Building a positive image of women by recognizing their contribution to the society, polity and the economy.
- Developing ability to think critically.
- Fostering decision making and action through collective process.
- Enabling women to make informed choices in areas like education, employment and health (especially reproductive health).
- Ensuring equal participation in developmental process.

- Providing information, knowledge and skill for economic independence.
- Enhancing access to legal literacy and information relating to their rights and entitlements in society with a view to enhance their participation on equal footing in all areas.

Women's Empowerment Year (2001)

The year 2001 was observed as the year of women's empowerment in order to create large scale awareness about women's rightful place in the mainstream of nation's development.

National Policy for the Empowerment of Women (2001)

A National Policy for the empowerment of women was announced on 20th March, 2001. The goal of this policy is to bring about the advancement, development and empowerment of women through the process of change in attitudes towards women, elimination of all forms of discrimination against women and active participation of women in all spheres of life, which will empower women both socially and economically.

National Curriculum Framework for School Education of NCERT (2005) and Girl's Education

National Curriculum Framework for School Education of NCERT (2005) also stresses the need of making education accessible to more and more girls, both in rural and urban areas. An emphasis is there on the need to develop and implement Gender Inclusive and Gender Sensitive curricular strategies. The National Curriculum Framework has come forward with a practical solution—education of both boys and girls. It suggests linking of education to life skills of both boys and girls.

Government Programmes on Women Education in India—Role of the Department of Women and Child Development

The department formulates plans, policies and programmes and enacts/amends legislation and co-ordinates the efforts of both governmental and nongovernmental organisations working to improve the condition of women and children in the country. The department has 4 autonomous organisations i.e. National Institute of Public Co-operation and Child Development (NIPCCD), Rastriya Mahila Kosh (RMK). Central Social Welfare Board (CSWB) and National Commission for Women (NCW).

Role of Central Social Welfare Board (CSWB)

The programmes implemented by the Central Social Welfare

Board include : socio-economic programme for needy/destitute women, condensed courses of education and vocational training courses for women and girls, awareness generation projects for rural and poor women, family counselling centres, holiday camps for children, welfare extension projects in border areas and balwadies, creches and hostels for working women.

Balika Samridhi Yojana

Balika Samridhi Yojana was launched in 1997 and aims to change the community's attitude towards the girls' child. The mother of a girl child born after August 15, 1997 in a family below poverty line is given a grant of Rs. 500 to be deposited in an interest bearing account of a financial institution in the name of girl child. In addition the girl child will become eligible for annual scholarships in each successfully completed year of schooling.

Adult Education Programme

Several adult education programmes have been undertaken in the country as Social Education (1951), Farmer's Functional Literacy Programme (1967), Non-formal Education (1978), National Literacy Mission (1988) and Total Literacy Campaign (1991) with a view to achieve Education for All by 2000 A.D. The National Literacy Mission came up with different plans and strategies.

Integrated Child Development Service (ICDS)

The programme of ICDS provides a package of services comprising supplementary nutrition, immunisation, health check up, referral services, preschool education, and health and nutrition education for the mothers. The target groups are children in the age group of 0-6 years and expectant women and nursing mothers.

The ICDS continues to be the major vehicle for attaining the goal of early childhood survival and their development. The ICDS network is being used for attaining the objectives of National Population Policy, 2000 also. In each ICDS Project, on average there are 140 Anganwadi Centres (AWCs).

The Mahila Samakhya Programme (1989)

The Mahila Samakhya Programme (1989) is working to create a demand for girls education in the states of Uttar Pradesh, Karnataka and Gujarat. The programme has helped women to address the larger socio-cultural issues that hindered the participation of girls in the education system.

District Primary Education Programme (DPEP) (1994)

The Government of India launched the District Primary Education Programme in 1994 in 271 districts of 18 states (Annual Report, MHRD, 2001-02). The programme has been started in low female literacy states and districts. In 1994 the Government had introduced universalization of Girl's Education Bill in the Parliament. It started to make education accessible to girls with all necessary support. DPEP intends to reduce overall dropout rates for all students and to reduce differences in enrolment.

Common Minimum Programmes

The provision of free and compulsory education for all children, until they complete the age of 14 is a directive principle of the constitution. While adopting the constitution in 1950, the goal was to provide free and compulsory education to all children upto the age of 14 by 1960. After this now the target year is 2010 to achieve the goal of universalisation of primary education under the common minimum programmes.

Sarva Siksha Abhiyan (SSA) (2000)

The Sarva Siksha Abhiyan was launched in the year 2000. This scheme seeks to bridge gender inequality by giving due emphasis on promoting education of girl child in the society and to afford them social justice, security and equity at par with the boy child. Under this scheme, the National Programme of Nutritional Support to Primary Education (Mid-Day Meal Scheme) and National Programme for Education of Girls at Elementary Level (NPEGEL) were implemented to provide additional support to education of girls at the elementary level. The programme motivates girls who are not attending school with the support of the community.

Natural Learning Experiences (NLE)

Natural Learning Experiences (NLE) and activity based learning help in improving teaching at school and the other learning process level. This type of teaching attracts children including girls to attend the school.

Education for ST Girls in Low Literacy Pockets

The scheme launched in 1993-94 aims at raising the literacy level of tribal females in 48 identified tribal districts of eight states with female literacy below 2 per cent.

Kanyashram

This centrally sponsored scheme was started in 1990-91 in

different states and UTs for the establishment of Kanyashrams for the education of ST girls.

Conclusion

Women education is a priority area. Women are to be educated in the search for a safe environment, economic and social justice, adequate reallocation of resources, the survival of all species and the common goal of healthy planet in which the future generation can flourish.

REFERENCES

Aggarwal, J.C. and Agarwal S.P., (1994), *Women's Education in India. Historical Review, Present Status and Perspective Plan with Statistical Indcators,* Concept Publishing Company, New Delhi.

Das, R., (2005), *"Education and Womens Empowernment",* in National Seminar on Women Education in Orissa, SB. Women's College, Cuttack, 15-16 Jan., 2005.

Das, R., (2006), *"Education and Empowment of Tribal Women",* in Tribal Development in India, (Ed., S.K. Mishra, A.K. Samal and B. Rath, Talcher College, Talcher.

Government of India, (1966), *Education and National Development, Report of the Education Commission (1964-66),* Ministry of Education, New Delhi.

Government of India, (1986), *National Policy on Education (1986),* Ministry of Human Resource Development, New Delhi.

Government of India, (1992), *National Policy on Education - Programme of Action (1992),* Ministry of Human Resource Development, New Delhi.

Government of India, (2003), *Tenth Five Year Plan (2002- 2007),* Planning Commission, New Delhi.

NCERT, (2005), *National Curriculum Framework for School Education (2005),* New Delhi.

15

ENHANCING THE STATUS OF WOMEN—Issues and Strategies

—PRAVAKAR MALLICK

Education is the corner stone of the women's empowerment because it enables them to respond to the opportunities, challenge their traditional roles and change their lives. Women education has a more significant impact on poverty and development than mans education. It is most influential factor in improving child health and reducing infant mortality. Women education also has an impact on family size. The more education a women has, the higher is the degree of her independence. Education would empower women to achieve social, psychological, economic and political dreams which are denied to her traditionally.

In India women enjoyed almost equal status with men during medieval era. The status of women went down considerably. The position of women in modern India has changed significantly, educationally, politically and legally. Inspite of constitutional guarantee, they face discrimination and marginalisation on various fields. Their life at home and outside still remain extremely monotonous. The female literacy rate which is 54.16 per cent (2001 census) is not a great achievement after sixty years of independence. Girl's enrollment in higher education is meagre i.e., 39.9 per cent. The major issues in the way of women education are population explosion, illiteracy and poor enrolment of girls in different stages. The percentage of girls enrolment to total enrollment in different stages has been depicted in Table 15.1.

The above table shows that since 1950-51 girls participation has increased mani-fold at different stages e.g. primary, middle, secondary/Hr.sec. and higher education level from 28.1% to 43.7% in primary level, 16.1% to 40.9%, 13.30% to 38.6% and 10.00%

to 39.4% respectively at secondary, higher secondary and higher education level. However, the girls participation is still below 50% at all stages of education.

Table 15.1 : Percentage of Girls Enrolment to Total Enrolment at Different Stages

Year	*Primary (I-V)*	*Secondary (VI-VIII)*	*Hr.Sec/ Intermediate (IX-XII)*	*Higher education/ Degree and above all level*
1950-51	28.1	16.1	13.3	10.0
1960-61	32.6	23.9	20.5	20.4
1970-71	37.4	29.3	25.0	23.2
1980-81	38.6	32.9	29.6	26.7
1990-91	41.5	36.7	32.9	33.3
2000-01	43.7	40.9	38.6	39.4

Source : Census of India (2001).

Today, women have realized that they cannot remain for ever confined to the kitchen and the four walls of room. They want to play multifaceted rolls to offset the challenges emerging out of the socio-economic changes taking place in the country. However, certain factors have hampered their success. They are i.e. lack of adequate finance, training facilities lack of awareness etc. Their talent and creativity need to be harnessed for their own development/empowerment and benefit of the society. The following are certain issues, which obstructs their development.

- Wide gender gaps in enrolment, attendance and retention.
- Biased parental attitude in bringing up girls child in family.
- Biased societal attitude, beliefs, traditions and customs, dogmas and superstitions etc.
- Low self-esteem and self-confidence among women.
- Resistance, shyness and conservatism in social system.
- Low participation of women in skill development training programme in rural areas.
- Lack of educational guidance and counselling centres in rural areas.
- Violence and sexual harassment against women in the society.

- Lack of knowledge among women about existing government scheme and programmes for promotion of girls education, development and empowerment.
- Lack of knowledge among masses about human rights-women rights, relelvant laws and law enforcing agencies.
- Lack of opportunities for girls and women to participate in decision making process.

Several programmes have been launched with the objective of empowering women. They are to be implemented by Government in collaboration with the NGOs and members of Community. Some of them are as follows :

Strategies

- Organization of gender sensitization programmers for community, teachers, policy personnel and health workers etc.
- Organization of awareness building programmes for girls and parents through Government schemes and programmes for social economical and political empowerment.
- Organization of programmes for providing opportunities to women for self-expression.
- Organization of awareness building programmes for women to promote their participation in skill development programmes.
- Exploration of possibilities of running diversified skill development training courses/trades for women in rural areas.
- Continued mobilization by conducting public awareness programmes on unequal and discriminatory treatment in socialization process of girls.
- Organization of gender sensitization programmes for teachers, community members, women groups such as Mahila Mandals, PTAs, MTAs in relation to girls education and empowerment.
- Development of motivational materials (print, electronic) focusing on the importance of educating women.
- Help to parents in getting their daughter enrolled.
- Provision of help line services for women.

- Strengthening adult literacy programmes in those districts and blocks where the literacy is below 10 per cent.
- Mass mobilization by creating public awareness, focusing on messages that women and men have for equal rights to participate in activities.
- Preparation of women for contesting Panchayat elections and exercise their rights.
- Reservation of women for admission in various courses.
- Introduction on new professional courses for women.
- Organization of career counselling for awareness of girls.
- Special training programmes for leadership development may be periodically organized for women in educational administration.

Conclusion

Today there is a great awakening among the women. Indian women have engaged themselves and trying to their best to become proficient in many activities and professions. With the adequate opportunities they will deliver best result with their strength i.e. tolerance, honesty, hardwork, co-operation, adjustment and dependence, determination and self-confidence.

The agenda of empowerment of women is simple. It will not get accomplished through legal and constitutional provisions. Women will gain power only when both men and women begin to respect and accept the contribution. Empowerment is on its way but a lot is yet to be achieved to realize in full capacity. The issues and reasons behind are not legal but structural and attitudinal. Education would surely liberate and equip women with ability to take control of their life, accomplish their dreams and enhance their status. It is noteworthy the opinion of President A.P.J. Abdul Kalam,– "Empowering women is a pre-requisite for creating a good nation, when women are empowered, society with stability is assured". Empowerment is essential as their thoughts and value systems lead to the development of good family, good society and ultimately a good nation.

REFERENCES

Begum, Mustiary, (2006), *Women Entrepreneurship in India,* University News, AIU House, Vol-44, No. 15, New Delhi.

Dhamija, N. and S. K. Panda, (2006), *Women Empowerment Through Education–Role of Universities,* University News, AIU House, Vol-44, No. 27, New Delhi.

Khanum, Bakhtenasar, (1999), *Status of Women in Indian Higher Education,* University News, AIU House, New Delhi.

Sharma, Seetal, (2006), *"Educated Women, Empowered Women"* Yojana, Govt. of India, Vol-50, No. 1, New Delhi.

Swain, S. K., (2000), *Trends and Issues in Education,* Kalyani Publishers, New Delhi.

16

THE NEED OF WOMEN EDUCATION

—JAYANTI SATRUSALLYA

Man has not questioned women's right to enter any field of activity but deliberately avoided and restricted her influence and scope of work in the name of rigid rules and customs. But education is the perfect agent of basic change in the status of women. An educated woman can well interact with her family on decision making, property matter, career choices etc. The sole aim of women education is Women Empowerment and Gender Equity. At Nairobi in 1985 the International Women's Conference was held where 'empowerment' was defined as" a distribution of social power and control of resources in favour of women'. Can this be achieved without proper education? Can a woman be recognized without education and awareness? Can she get economic independence and freedom of choice without being educated? The above questions are to be answered for which lot of explorations are in-evitable.

Need of Women Education

Women-education is essential to maintain a sustainable growth in our society. Many things have been discussed by educationists. Still we have not reached a final conclusion on the matter. Development of women through reservation in all spheres except State Assembly and Parliament has become the conclusion. We are facing difficulties and trying to find out some suitable solutions and planning for avoidance of such occurrences in future. We must have to wake up and start preparing a future model of sustained development for our country.

Lack of proper vision and fighting among political leaders has not given us actual benefit. However, we have already faced two revolutions of agriculture and industry and now going through the knowledge revolution where knowledge is shared by one and all. Government in Centre and State are completely aware of the role of both male and female in this revolutionary process. But there is a gender disparity. It causes check on the growth. Hence there is a gap between the concept and the solution. Knowing and doing are two different things. The male dominated society has already realized the need of women's education, their effect, utility but not wholly prepared to accept it and do something more on this line. It causes social imbalance. The age old traditional formula of not educating girls will not continue any more. Cultural and State legislations have came to the forefront. Women empowerment is possible only when those legislations will be perfectly materialized. Can we use these acts without proper awareness? Awareness is a long term affair for which education is essential. Let us mention some of the Acts meant for protection of women.

- The Moral Traffic (Prevention) Act, 1956
- The Maternity Benefit Act, 1961
- The Dowry Prohibition Act, 1961
- Indecent Representation of Women (Prohibition) Act, 1986
- Protection of Women from Domestic Violence Act, 2005.

The women of India constitute 48.3% of the total population. It clearly indicates that remaining 52% male cannot give us complete economy, polity and other developments. Hence Gender Equity is a must for our society. A ground must have to be prepared for acceptance of the concept of girls education.

Brief History of Girls Education in Pre-Independence Period

During the pre-independence period education was restricted to women of the ruling families and Brahmins. The Devadasis and Vaishnavis were also getting education for spread of Vaishnovism. Later on during the administration of East India Company in 1825, The Calcutta Ladies School was started for Indian women. Due to constant effort of Britishers by the end of 1829 the number of Girl's School reached 30 and 354 by the year 1850 with an enrolment of 11,500 girls. Despite of such growth rate in girls education the Hunter Report (1881) mentioned regarding poor ratio of girl students. It was six girls in every 100 boys in Primary schools. It suggested for different curriculum for girls students to attract them. In 1863 Brahmo Samaj started correspondence education for girls and named the mission as "Antahpur Shiksha" which attracted large number of married women to get education. Gradually women education became an wave and the first women's college was established in Lucknow in 1901 named as Women's Christian College and subsequently first Women University was established in 1916 at Mumbai named as Shrimati Nathibai Damodar Thakersey (SNDT) University. Now the number has been increased to a satisfactory number. 39.94 per cent women are continuing their higher studies in 1578 women's colleges and 5 women universities and in other institutions of higher studies.

Women Education in the Present Context

Women play double role of earning for family and caring for the children. Because of poverty in India those women often lack education which adds problem to it. There is a link between education and development. Education helps in enhancing women's income, social respect, family care, etc. But there are still some social causes for which girls are deprived of proper education. Even though some girls are admitted to the schools, there is a high dropout rate among girls, specifically among rural girls. The causes may be listed as:

1. Need of girls in the farms or family occupation or responsibility of looking after younger ones.
2. Parents are sometimes unable to bear educational expenses.
3. Parents do not want their girls when school continues until dark.
4. Loss of girl's time in her absence in the family is counted as a direct loss to the family.
5. Some schools are inadequate to accommodate the difficulties of girls when she reaches puberty due to lack of sanitation facility.

Due to adoption of various programmes by Union Government like Education For All, Sarva Siksha Abhiyan, Kasturba Gandhi Balika Vidyalaya the rate of girls education has been raised from 8.86 per cent in 1951 to 54.16 per cent in 2001. A number of special drives in respect of literacy promotion like Farmer's Functional Literacy Programme, Mass Programme for Functional Literacy, Total Literacy Campaign, Operation Black Board etc, have been introduced where Women's Literacy been given priority. Mere Literacy is not enough rather Higher Education has become acute necessity.

Research has shown that educating girls offers a multitude of benefits to them, their families and the society. It has become helpful to women folk to participate more meaningfully in Political and Civil life. It improves overall, conomic growth and leads to greater care of the environment. Society can have a more productive work force through engagement of women in enhancing knowledge and skill. It will also fight against poor child health, low educational performance of the successors and higher fertility and ultimately in reducing gender inequality.

Education of women is an effective means to counter gender discrimination. It is a powerful weapon to fight against malnutrition. It influences her nutritional status as well as her family. Education empowers women to make and take decisions about themselves, their families and communities. President A.P.J. Abdul Kalam has rightly said,– "Empowering women is a pre-requisite for creating a good nation. When women are empowered, society with stability is assured. Empowerment of women is essential as their thoughts and their value systems lead to the development of a good family, good society and ultimately a good nation."

Women empowerment has invited women's participation in vocational, technical and professional education at various level. The most welcomed fact that the National Commission for Women was setup by an act of Parliament in 1990 to safeguard the rights and legal entitlements of women.

The 73rd and 74th amendments (1993) to the Constitution of India have provided for reservation of seats in the local bodies of Panchayats and Municipalities for women. Can we call it complete unless they are proportionately represented in State Assembly and Parliament.? The demand can be achieved when proper empowerment of women will be possible. Women's education is the only solution to it. No girl should be left out of the educational institution until she reaches the age of twenty. Continuous engagement of girls in educational institutions through incentives for a longer period of a time will certainly help the nation to achieve its goal by 2020.

It is an encouraging fact that there is more and more girls enrollment in higher education. They are now capturing a good number of administrative, software and managerial position. Still is it not a fact that though woman has acquired an economic and social identity she is forced to quit her job in the name of being a responsible mother or sister or wife and so on.? Time has come to think of women education seriously.

Women Education : Ultimate Vision

Women is the cornerstone of women empowerment. More effort is required in this area. Proper education will empower her socially, psychologically, economically and politically.

Special support services like higher incentives to the parents of enrolled girls effective implementation of mid-day meals programme, more and more skill development courses for girls should also be introduced. Innovative programmes, lower cost, offering of stipend and involvement of NGOs will certainly add success to this effort.

WOMEN'S ACCESS TO HIGHER EDUCATION IN ORISSA —Issues and Initiatives

—ARATI SATPATHY

Introduction

In the words of the Indian Education Commission (1964 - 66),– "For full development of our human resources, the improvement of homes and for moulding the character of the children during the most impressionable years of infancy, the education of women is of even greater importance than that of man".

Access to education has been recognised as a fundamental right of both men and women. The educational background of a woman has a direct bearing on her development. Unless women have participation in social, political and scientific/technological fields, we can not conceive of national progress. Their progress is very often equated with the nation's progress and therefore their participation in developmental activities of the society is always an imperative.

Education as an Instrument for Empowering Women

The empowering role of woman's education is multipronged affecting not only every aspect of women's lives, but also the lives of their children and others who are likely to depend on them.

Education has the potential of empowering women in several ways :

- by equipping them with the awareness and knowledge required to make beneficial life choices.

- by increasing their ability to access resources and services.
- by enabling them to become informed consumers and citizens.
- by inculcating a feeling of self-worth.
- and by increasing their ability to challenge and make
- accountable to those who hold power and authority etc.

Any discussion on equity of access to educational opportunities at the highest level must begin by recognising the processes of exclusion at various stages of education. The prevailing educational system denies opportunities to vast sections of the population both men and women. But when the figures are examined from the standpoint of gender equity, it becomes apparent that women are specially disadvantaged. The data on educational access reveals that barely 54.16% women in the country are literate. In 2001, rural and urban female literacy rates are 47.22% and 72.68% respectively. The gap between the rural male-female as well as urban male female is again of not only gender disparity but also of the uneven spread of resources over rural and urban areas. The female literacy gap across urban rural region is 25.46% as per 2001 census figures, which imply that resource allocation, utilisation and proper management of the literacy programmes have benefited the urban women more than the rural women.

The UGC's Tenth Plan profile shows the growth of student enrolment (both formal and informal) had increased in the last decade from 62.17 lakhs in 1992-93 to 93.14 lakhs in 1999-2000 (i.e. 50% increase); but women's enrolment had not risen proportionately to that of men (UGC, 2001). Although women's enrolment increased from 20.92 lakhs to 33.24 lakhs, it represented marginal improvement, from 33.6% in 1992-93 to 36.15% in 2000, indicating access to higher education, the document further stated that India's parameters were approximately one-sixth of developed countries.

Women in Orissa—Status and Prospect

Orissa has a total number of 45 government degree colleges. Out of these 16 are women's 29 are co-ed. All these government colleges have a sanctioned strength of 16,194 seats in the Science, Arts and Commerce streams. The 16 women's government degree colleges have 3,600 numbers of sanctioned strength exclusively for women in the streams of Science, Arts and Commerce.

There are 8 universities in the state offering higher education to the students at post graduation level. The premier ones are universities of Utkal, Sambalpur, Berhampur, cultural and university of Agriculture and Technology.

The sanctioned student strength in Utkal University is 1155 excluding the sponsored courses with 223 seats at M.Phil. level. Though the presence of girls in these universities is more than 60% their participation is restricted to stereotyped discipline. On the other hand in science and computer education only 20% girls are studying. Employment scope is very restricted.

Professional courses are available to girls in the polytechnics and ITIs. Besides the above, there is only 30% reservation for girls in the Engineeing colleges of the state.

The number of females registered their names in different employment exchanges in the state is 20,487 against 1,30,586 persons registered in total. Highest number of females have registered in Bhubaneswar exchange followed by Cuttack and Rourkela exchanges.

Women employment in Orissa is highest in Primary sector (more than 80%) and increasing day by day while their participation in secondary sector or in industrial activities is declining. In tertiary or service sector their participation has increased marginally by 0.46% during the period of 1981-91. Most of them work as agricultural labourers, whereas most of the males work as cultivators in this sector. It indicates slow expansion of girls higher education.

Why there is Slow Expansion in Higher Education of Girls ?

There are certain serious difficulties in the way of expansion of girls education. Some of these are :

- Tradition-ridden social customs, poverty, early marriage in rural areas.
- Conservative attitude of parents, lack of incentives.
- Shortage of Women teachers, lack of hostel and school buildings, inadequate transportation and blind believes.

Expected Initiatives

There is no dispute that at government level some well thought planning has been made to meet these challenges. Education commissions have suggested some viable measures from time to time. Feedback and inputs from the field study are also being accepted. But considering the exigencies of women education in this changed social ambience, certain initiatives have to be undertaken. These are :

- Provision for separate schools for girls in each area.
- Appointment of women teachers in primary schools.
- Attachment of nursery or pre-primary school to every girls' school.
- Appointment of school mothers.
- Adequate remuneration to women teachers.
- Participation of NGOs in spreading women education.
- Part-time eduction programmes.
- Job-oriented post elementary education.
- More incentives to S.C. & S.T. girl students.

Conclusion

Since education is one of the most important media through which knowledge and information is acquired, a nation and for that matter a state can not afford to marginalise it. During these fifty years of post-independent era our experience is that we have not been able to keep pace with other developed countries because of apalling scene of backwardness of the women. In all most all advanced countries the women education is at par with the education of the man. India in this regard is lagging behind others. In this globalised age, the first impediment which we should fight is social inequity. Lack of women education is certainly the most vulnerable of social inequities. Hence we must have rethinking to be aware of the emerging issues concerning women education and their desired status in the society.

REFERENCES

Economic and Political Weekly, A Semeeksha Trust Publication, Jan 15-21, 2005, Vol. XL, No. 3

A Situational Analysis of Women in Orissa School of Women's Studies, Utkal University, Bhubaneswar.

Kochhar, S.K., : *Pivotal Issues in Indian Education.*

18

STATUS OF WOMEN EDUCATION IN INDIA —A Reflection

—NILADRI PRADHAN

Introduction

Education is a pre-requisite for progress and development. In India, education has been accorded a high priority as an integral part of country's developmental process. Today the main thrust of educational activities is towards promotion of quality, quantity and excellence at different stages of education, it is a very grim situation that today still we have many illiterates than what our population was at the time of independence in 1947. In our journey to progress and development, the first step should naturally be in the area of women education as women constitute half of the human population. In a world where socio-economic development is becoming more knowledge intensive the role of education becomes more crucial. Therefore the need of the hour is to concentrate, on reforming, reorienting, rejuvenating and revitalising the entire education system to meet the emerging need and challenges of the new millennium.

The constitution of India has guaranteed the right to equality to all its citizens irrespective of their sex, caste, creed, and religion. Indian democracy, right from the days of independence, has been thriving on these basic principles for the last five decades. The national movement under the leadership of Mahatma Gandhi was one of the first attempt to draw Indian women out of the restricted circles of domestic life into equal role with men. Writing in "Young India" in 1918, Gandhiji said, woman is the companion of man gifted with equal mental capacities. She has the right to participation in the minutest details of the activities of man. She has the same right of freedom and liberty as his.

Historical Review

In India women education was encouraged in ancient days. Hence we find mention of numerous learned women in vedic and upanishadic periods. But situation changed during the muslim period. The women were sent behind purdah under the Muslim influence and the unsafe condition prevailed in their society. But by the middle of the nineteenth century, some progressive Indians and Englishmen started working for their reawakening. This encouraged development of their education.

Present status of women education in India is comparatively high. Today women are showing an interest for professional education. Girls show special inclination towards fashion designing, hotel management, airlines, teaching etc. The girls are also attracted towards various courses, such as medical, engineering and nursing. With the help of higher education women can reach the top positions. We can mention the names of Kalpana Chowla first Indian woman went to space, Kiran Bedi, the first lady I.P.S. officer in India and first woman to receive the magsaysay award Mrs. Vijaylaxmi Pandit, first Indian lady president of General Assembly of the U.N.O. Minister of U.P. Moreover Indira Gandhi first lady Prime Minister of India and first woman to receive Bharat Ratna. Now Indian women are forced to earn money in addition to slogging away at home.

Women Empowerment

Empowerment is a multi-dimensional process, which should enable the individuals or a group of individuals to realize their full identity and powers in all spheres of life. It consists of greater access to knowledge and resources, greater autonomy in decision making to enable them to have greater ability to plan their lives, or have greater control over circumstances that influence their lives and free them from the shackles imposed on them by custom, belief and practice. Empowerment of women also means equal status to women. Empowering women socio-economically through increased awareness of their rights and duties as well as access to resources is a decisive step towards greater security for them. Empowerment includes higher literacy level and education for women, better health care for women and children, equal ownership of productive resources, increased participation in economic and commercial sectors, awareness of their rights and responsibilities, improved standards of living and acquiring 'self-reliance, self-esteem and self-confidence'.

M.K. Gandhi had said that 'men and women are equal in status but not identical'. It is an active, multi-dimensional process which enables women to realize their potential, identity and power in order to raise their status. Power cannot be transacted but has to be acquired, sustained and preserved. Women have to become conscious of their oppression, grab opportunities and take leadership and become self-reliant.

Women Empowerment and Planning Process

All round development of women has been one of the focal points of planning process in India. The First Five-Year Plan (1951-56) envisaged a number of welfare measures for women. Establishment of the Central Social Welfare Board (CSWB), organization of mahila mandals or women's clubs and the community development programmes were a few steps in this direction. In the second five year plan (1956-61), the empowerment of women was closely linked with the overall approach of intensive agricultural development programmes. The third and fourth, five year plans (1961-66 and 1969-74) supported female education as a major welfare measure. The fifth five-year plan (1974-79) emphasised training of women, who were in need of income and protection. Functional literacy programmes got priority. This plan coincided with International Women's Decade and the submission of report of the committee on the status of women in India. In 1976, Women's Welfare and Development Bureau was set up under the ministry of Social Welfare. It was to act as a nodal point to co-ordinate policies and programmes for women's development.

The sixth five year plan (1980-85) saw a definite shift from welfare to development. It recognized women's lack of access to resources as a critical factor impending their growth. The seventh plan (1985-90) emphasised the need for gender equality and empowerment. For the first time, emphasis was placed upon qualitative aspects such as inculcation of confidence, generation of awareness with regard to rights and training in skills for better employment. The eighth five year plan (1992-97) focused on empowering women, especially at the grassroot level, through panchayati raj institutions. The ninth five year plan (1995-2000) adopted a strategy of women's component plan, under which not less than 30 per cent of funds/benefits were earmarked for women-specific programmes. The tenth plan (2002-07) approach aims at empowering women through translating the recently adopted National Policy for Empowerment of Women (2001) into action and ensuring survival, protection and development of women and children through rights based approach.

Committees and Commissions on Women

- Report of the Durgabai Deshmukh Committee on Education of Women (1959) made comprehensive suggestions and became a policy document guiding the subsequent five year plan formulation. The need for undifferentiated curricula for both boys and girls was highlighted to treat education of girls as a special problem.
- Undifferentiated curricula upheld by Hansa Mehta Committee (1964) Education Commission (1964-66), National Policy on Education (1986) and reiterated strongly in the NPE (1986) revised in 1992 and its programme of Action
- The Report of the Committee on Status of Women Towards Equality,1974, revealed declining proportion of women in the population, low female literacy and education, higher female mortality, waning economic participation and poor representation of women in political processes.
- The UN Development Decade (1975-85) saw growth of institutional mechanisms such as the Department of Women and Child Development, women's development corporations, integrating women in the mainstream, development of women and children in rural area; women as special groups for poverty removal, skill development TRYSEM, ICDS. Movement from welfare to development and finally to empowerment in the eighth plan.
- The National Perspective Plan for Women (1988-2000) chalked out the national gender agenda till the turn of the century with a strong focus on rural and disadvantaged women.
- Ramamurthy Review Committee: Towards an Enlightened and Humane Society underscored the need for redistribution of educational opportunities in favour of girls belonging to rural and disadvantaged sections with adequate support services (water, fodder, fuel, child care) and also asked for 50% share for girls in educational resources.
- The National Policy on Women's Empowerment (2001).

The goal of this policy is to bring about the advancement of women. Specifically, the objectives of this policy include:

- Creating an environment through positive economic and special policies for full development of women to enable them to realize their full potential;
- The dejure and de-facto enjoyment of all human rights and fundamental freedom by women on equal basis with men in all spheres-political, economic, social, cultural and Civil;
- Equal access to participation and decision making of women in social, political and economic life of nation;
- Equal access to women to health care, quality education at all levels, career and vocational guidance, employment, equal remuneration, occupational health and safety, social security and public office;
- Strengthening legal systems aimed at elimination of all forms of discrimination against women;
- Changing societal attitudes and community practices by active participation and involvement of both men women;
- Mainstreaming of discrimination and all forms of violence against women and the girl child; and
- Building and strengthening partnerships with civil society, particularly women's organizations.

Constitutional Provisions and Important Laws in India Affecting Women

- The equal remuneration Act of 1976 provides for equal pay to men women for equal work.
- Hindu Adoption and Maintenance Act, 1956 male or female Hindu having legal capacity, can take a son or daughter.
- The 73rd and 74th constitutional amendments (1992) give 33% representation to women in Panchayats and Nagar Palikas and 30% headships to women in these bodies at the village, block and district levels in rural areas and towns and cities.
- Article -14 confers on men and women equal rights and opportunities in political, economic and social spheres.

- Article 15(3) enables the state to make positive discrimination in favour of women.
- Article 39 (a) provides that the state shall direct policies towards securing for both men and women the right to adequate means of livelihood.
- Article 51 (a) (e) imposes a fundamental duty to renounce practices derogatory to the dignity of women.

International Convention

On 10th December 1948, the General Assembly of the United Nations adopted and proclaimed the Universal Declaration of Human Rights. It provides a common standard of achievement for all peoples and all nations. On 18th December 1979, the convention on the elimination of forms of discrimination against women was adopted by the United Nations Assembly.

Women Leadership

Generally leadership refers to one who leads way/path to people. Realizing the felt needs of local empowerment in 1992, the 73rd amendment was promulgated to provide the first step towards decentralization of powers at the grass root level. Panchayats, after the historic 73rd amendment, were made the smallest unit of governance with financial and political autonomy. Through the amendment women were also given a chance to lead. Leadership plays an important role in shaping the socio-economic and political structure of any society. It is the utmost responsibility of every leader to work for the welfare of people. Panchayati Raj institution is one of the most important political innovations of independent India. Leadership in the context of Panchayati Raj institution has great importance as the objective constituting local governance was to encourage leadership according to developmental needs of countryside. Effective functioning of Panchayati Raj institutions depends primarily on the quality of leadership available at the grass root level.

Schemes for Women's Entrepreneurship

The Government has introduced many development and welfare programmes for women. These programmes are aimed at providing financial and technical assistance to poor women to start self- employment units. Integrated Rural Development Programme (IRDP),Training of Rural Youth for Self Employment, (TRYSEM) now renamed as Swarna Jayanti Gram Swarozgar Yojana (SGSY), Socio-Economic Programme (SEP), Support to Training and

Employment Programme (STEP), Development of Women and Children (DWC), are some of the important programmes implemented by the Government with reference to women's development. Like wise women's development corporation, Central Social Welfare Board and State Social Welfare Board are also entrusted with women development schemes through financial assistance and generate employment for women.

Conclusion

For making women's education popular school going should be made convenient and acceptable for girls special incentives should be given to women teachers. So, distinguished and great scholar, S.Radhakrishnan said 'There can not be educated people without educated women'. Our P.M. Pandit J. Nehru said that the most reliable indicator of a country's character is the status and social position of women more than anything else. Further mother is the pivot of family life in India. Our way of life depends on her. Awareness need to be generated among the masses regarding the necessity of educating girls, so as to prepare them to contribute effectively in the socio-economic development of the country to strengthen their role in the society and to realize their own capacities. Maximum mobilization of human and material resources for qualitative and quantitative development of women through formal and non-formal approach will go a long way in women empowerment. A strong will and ditermination with whole hearted support of all concerned in education of girls are urgently felt and essentially inevitable for bringing the vital section of the society to the mainstream of thc national development. Education of a boy is education of one person but education of girl is the education of entire family. J. Nehru has aptly enunciated that in order to awaken the people, it is the women who has to be awakened. Once she is on the move the household moves the village moves, the country moves and thus we build the India of tomorrow.

REFERENCES

Knight, L.W., (2004), *Educating Women Worldwide*, New Frontiers in Education,Vol-1, No. 1, New Delhi.

Peerzade, S.A., (2005), "Empowerment of Women: A Study", A Journal on Rural Development, *Kurukshetra*, New Delhi.

Pradhan, N., (2005), "Women Education: An Emerging Issue", *Ram-Eesh Journal of Education*, Vol 11, No. 2, Greater Noida.

19

"WOMEN EMPOWERMENT IN INDIA —Some Maladies and Remedies"

—SRIKANT KUMAR PAIKRAY

It is true, the mighty strength that lies behind the man is woman. It is true, the status of women is a test of civilization. It is true, the level of civilization can be measured only by the degree of freedom, respect and role given to women, and it is also true, women are recognized as 'power' and accordingly be included actively in the process of development of a society. So empowerment is a 'need of the hour' and the 20th century is marked as the beginning of the process. Again it is a right time to repeat the golden words of Swami Vivekananda, "Arise and Awake" to the women of the world for want of empowerment and for this they would have raise their voice for Quality, Dignity and Self-respect.

Women Empowerment is being recognized globally as a key element of progress and prosperity. Empowerment of women simply means to give power and freedom in all spheres so that they can contribute immensely for the progress of the society and for the nation. Education is widely assumed to be a fundamental pre-requisite for participation in the advanced sectors of society. Higher skills, greater information and knowledge are essential for administration, improvement in productivity, and citizenship in a modern democracy. Great hopes have been pinned on education of girls to bring about social change towards modernization. Education not only enables her to adjust to changes already taking place but it is the means whereby he/she can accelerate such changes. Third World Countries hold as an axiom that education will result changes in values and attitudes conducive to development.

Some Maladies

It is significantly found that a large number of women continue to be bound by traditional practices and conventions. They fail to realize that these have become obsolete and are an obstacle to progress. Development in the true sense has not reached the women, who constitute nearly 50% of the county's human resources. Gender has been an important divide of people in almost all societies through out the ages. It has divided people into two largest groups, determining their values. Thus, it is expected that the male would be dominant, ambitious, achievement-oriented and master of the home and society at large, while the female should be passive, obedient and followers of the male. A life of freedom, openness, achievement belonged to the male while a life of dependence, confinement is of the female. Women have been denied freedom, positive share in social and political power, right to individuality, just because they are women; they belong to a particular gender.

Gender equity is a pre-requisite for effective participation of women in strengthening the structure of democracy. Women have been marginalized because of several socio-economic and political constraints. Despite the fact that India has a strong written constitution proclaiming laws for equality and welfare of women, barbaric and savagist practices still continue to haunt women in the form of female foeticide, female infanticide, child labour, child marriage, rape, sexual harassment, gender inequality, molestation, eva-teasing, forced prostitution, child pornography etc. The condition of an Indian widow is quite deplorable as she is despised by her family as well as by the society.

Some research studies realise that the problems faced by women are multidimensional and multi faceted which affect the social, psychological, economic political life and status of women in Indian society. Some are discussed below.

Low Female Literacy

Education is the sine-qua-non of progress of a society and it has been an important and integral part of social and cultural life. But, there is a significant hiatus between Male and Female literacy rate. The gender gaps in literacy can be ascribed to the general attitude and social perceptions of giving lower precedence to girls education. If we analyze the census report of India we can very well mark that the female literacy stands constantly lower than the literacy rate of males as shows the table below.

Table 19.1 : Literacy Rate of India

S.No.	*Census Period*	*Male*	*Female*	*Total*
1.	1981	46.82	24.82	32.23
2.	1991	64.01	39.03	52.01
3.	2001	75.85	54.16	65.38

Source: Statistical Abstract of India 2002.

High Proportion of Women in Primary Sector

Women constitute an important segment of the labour force. Women folk play a vital role in primary sector of the countries' economy. The unorganized primary sector which includes agriculture, animal husbandry, fishery, forestry, mining and quarrying, plantations and allied activities, absorbs as much as 74% of the total female workers. The female workers are engaged significantly in the marginal occupations such as collection of wood, fish, cow dung, fetching drinking water, maintenance of kitchen gardens, tailoring, weaving etc. But it is found that there are low representation of women employees in the organized sector only 14.3 during 2004. The unpaid economic activities of women and their contribution in the domestic sector remain un-reported and go largely unrecognized.

Un-equal Remuneration

There is significant inequality in earning income by the women from the same type of work particularly in the unorganized sector. Though Equal Remuneration Act, 1976 is in force tlll date, there is gross violation of the Act by the private sector organizations and employers of unorganized sector. Though implementation of the Act is enforced through inspections, detection and prosecutions, these cases are too inadequate compared to the number of women working in the unorganized sector.

Deficiencies in Health and Nutrition

Indian women are generally deficient in some essential nutrition requirements like vitamins, iron and protein. Traditionally, male members of the family were the first eaters and female members were the last to eat. There is a direct correlation between parent's education and health, nutritional status of girls children. Higher the parent's education, greater the percentage of girls being healthy. However, nutritional status during adolescence determines the health of women. Regardless of their health and body pattern, Indian women have always tried to bear children. Motherhood is considered a God's grace and signifies perfection in women's life. Normally, the health of a woman deteriorates during pregnancy and after child birth.

Crime against Women

Women, as physically weaker, have been subjected to various crimes, harassment and torture by dominant men groups. The occurrence of crimes like-rape, sexual abuse, molestation, kidnapping, abduction, dowry death, various types of torture and immoral trafficking etc. are against women in every now and then. Due to what, they feel depressed, frustrated and exhibit lack of confidence. The Crime Branch of Police, Government of Orissa and Human Rights Protection Cell reported some cases of crimes and violence against women in Orissa for the past six years (1997-2002) which indicate, that these cases are continuously increasing and they, therefore need more care and protection.

Table 19.2 : Reported Crimes against women in Orissa

Sl.No.	*Types of Crime*	*1997*	*1998*	*1999*	*2000*	*2001*	*2002*
1.	Rape	633	798	816	753	790	691
2.	Molestation	1373	1918	1555	1681	1655	1605
3.	kidnapping	405	446	429	358	435	432
4.	Dowry deaths	324	387	382	448	448	418
5.	Non-dowry torture	413	499	427	452	452	524
6.	Immoral Trafficking	11	11	26	18	18	24

Source: Crime Branch of Police, Govt. of Orissa.

Some Remedies

There was a time when every woman reaching marriageable age was assured of husband, home and security. Women outside the family had no refuge. The profession of the women was fixed to kitchen and household works which was continued by succeeding generations. Social mobility was slight, and tight. But today it all changed. The conventional society to which they belonged has been destroyed. There have been improvements in several domains of women's activity. More and more women are entering into the different "world of work" i.e. factories, homes, offices, shops, farms, teaching profession, nursing, medical engineering and the like. It is also significantly found that a large number of women are sole breadwinners and heads of their families.

Gradually, women have been empowered in social, political, economic, cultural, intellectual, educational, psychological and physical fields. Various laws have been formulated for the protection of women. A bulk of strategy has been geared to political and economic agenda. Considering, women as a vulnerable and disadvantaged group, efforts have been made to accord greater political and economic opportunity than given in the past. Some are given below.

National Prospective Plan for Women Education (1988-2000)

For empowering women in the social, cultural, economic political and educational fields the national plan has suggested the following:

- Awareness needs to be generated to educate girls to realize their roles in the society.
- Involvement of local leaders, voluntary organizations in the process of educating women.
- Need of opening more colleges and polytechnics for girls especially in rural areas.
- Provision of free ship and scholarship to girls for their higher studies.
- Girls should be encouraged to enter professional courses.
- Establishment of Guidance and counseling service centers for girls in the college.
- Reservation of 30% seats for girls in higher education.
- Vocational and technical education for women both formal and non-formal.
- Provision for part time study and correspondence courses for girls.

Tenth-Five Year-Plan

In order to create, greater employment avenues for women both in organized and unorganized sector it has been proposed to take the following measures during the tenth plan period.

- Elimination of gender bias in recruitment and improving working conditions for women employees.

- Organization of women's associations in the form of societies to enable them to get part time employment in the productive sector.
- Exploration of areas of employment for women.
- Provision of vocational training in various periods.
- Improvement of health and nutritional status of children below the age of six years.
- Reduction of incidence of infant and child mortality and malnutrition.

Anti-Poverty Programmes

A series of Legislation have been enacted from time to time for raising the socio-economic status of women in the country. A number of anti-poverty programmes and rural employment programmes which include the JRY, EAS, IRDP, DWCRA, TRYSEM, SITRA, GKY and MWS have been launched by the Central Government as well as by the state Government. Since April 1999 the JRY and EAS have been integrated and renamed as Jawahar Gram Samridhi Yojana (JGSY) and the rest six programmes have been integrated into Swarna Jayanti Gram Swarojgar Yojana (SGSY).

The SWA-SHAKTI Project

The objective of the project is to establish Women's Self Help Groups, which will develop linkage amongst the leading institutions to access credit facilities for women. The SWA-SHAKTI Project is financed by the Joint Collaboration of International Fund for Agricultural Development (IFAD) and International Development Association (IDA). In March 2001, it was launched in Orissa with a mission, empowering women through formation and promotion of one lakh Women Self-Help Groups (WSHG) by 2005 and strengthening of the existing ones. Accordingly the Women Self Help Groups are engaged in different types of economic activities such as horticulture, piggery, goatery, dairy, poultry, collection of forest products, broom making, basket making, handloom weaving etc.

Integrated Child Development Scheme (ICDS)

The scheme of Integrated Child Development Services is being implemented in different states of the country with a view to provide a package of services covering supplementary nutrition, immunization, pre-school education, health check up, nutrition and health education for women. The Kishori Shakti Yojana (KSY) is a special programme designed for adolescent girls in the age group of 11 to 18 years also comes under ICDS Programmes.

Panchayati Raj (a Political Empowerment)

Our constitution is 73rd Amendment Act, 1992 categorically provided for empowerment of rural women in the Panchayati Raj system in a more comprehensive manner. 30% seats have been reserved for women's representation at grassroot level political bodies. Such a move is aimed at mobilizing the effective participations of rural women in decision-making and implenentation of rural welfare programmes. Political empowerment of women allowed to continue in the true sense of the term will not only be a stepping stone in change of status of rural women so also it will create creative leadership and accelerate the pace of rural development.

National Curriculum Frame Work (NCF) 2005

The formal approach of equality of treatment, in terms of equal access or equal representation for girls, is inadequate. Today, there is a need to adopt a substantive approach, towards equality of outcome, where diversity, differences and disadvantages are taken into account. A critical function of education for equality is to enable all learners to claim their rights as well as to contribute for the society and the polity. We need to recognize that rights and choices in themselves cannot be exercised until central human capabilities are fulfilled. Thus, in order to make it possible for marginalized learners, and especially girls, to claim their rights as well as play an active role in shaping collective life, education must empower them to overcome the disadvantages of unequal socialization and enable them to develop their capabilities of becoming autonomous and equal citizens.

A Movement of Role-Reverse

Now a moment has come to reverse the role of women in our society. See the example of a household with various members of the family performing different tasks. The reverse role is that the father is cooking, the mother is fixing a tube light, the daughter returning from school on a bicycle, and the son milking a cow, the other sister climbing a mango tree, and the other son sweeping the floor. The grand father sewing on a button and the grandmother is doing the account'. So it is a symbol of shifting tasks and reverse roles to empower women in the present context.

REFERENCES

F.M. Sahoo, (1999), "Empowering Women: A Behavioral Analysis," *Vision*, Vol. XVIIl, No. 3-4, BBSR, India.

S. Venkataiah, (2001), *Women Education*, Anmol Publication and Pvt. Ltd. Ansari Road, Daryaganj, New Delhi.

Mira Seth, (2001), *Women and Development: The Indian Experience*, Sage Publications, New Delhi.

P.K. Ray, (2001), "Gender Inequality in Rural Power", *Vision*, VolXX, Nos. 3-4, BBSR, India.

Tenth Plan 2002-07, (2002), Orissa, Vols. 1 & 11, Govt. of Orissa.

Usha Devi, (2002), "Gender Equity in Higher Education", *Edutracks*, Vol. 2, No. 4, Neel Kamal Publication, Hyderabad.

M.V. Warlu, (2005), "Women Empowerment: A Prospective", *Vision*, Vol. XXV, Nos. 3-4, BBSR, India.

National Curriculum Framework - 2005. NCERT, New Delhi.

N. Panda, (2006), "Gender Development: A Compulsion to Counter Coverture", *Vision*, Vol. XXVI, No. 3, BBSR, India.

"WOMEN'S EDUCATION IN ANCIENT INDIA —A Rethinking

—BRUNDABAN PATRA

Introduction

Every enquiry of ancient Indian education goes back to the Vedic period, Vedas are self-revealed and others being originated later from them. They are the ways and means of achieving the spiritual goal of life; the Purusartha Chatustaya.[1] The equivalent words of education in Sanskrit are Vidya Shiksha, and Jnana. According to A.S. Alteker from Vedic age downwards the central concept of the Indians have been that it is a source of illumination giving us a correct lead in the various spheres of life.[2] Knowledge is the third eye of man which makes him capable to see the real object.[3] Upanishad says education is for liberation.[4] It nourishes us like the mother, directs us to the right path like the father and gives us pleasure and removes our pain like the wife. It is just like a desire-yielding tree that fulfills our desire.[5]

The status of women was held high during the Vedic period. According to scriptures women were regarded as Goddess, the embodiment of Shakti. They were worshiped as the symbol of fertility.[6] A sincere attempt has been made in this paper to discuss in details' about women education in ancient India. The topic covers from the Vedic period to the Buddhist period.

System of Education

There was Gurukula system of education in the Vedic period. Teacher was regarded as Guru or Acharya. Education of the students started with Upanayana ceremony. The ceremony was continued for three days. During these days the Guru holds the disciple within him as in a womb impregnates him with his spirit and delivers him in a new birth.[7] After the ceremony the students emerges as a Brahmachary and the teacher is designated as his spiritual and intellectual father.

Upanayana of Girls

Without undergoing upanayana samskara, nobody can recite Vedic mantras or offer Vedic sacrifices. It was obligatory for the girls to undergo upanayana.[8] Even Manu has mentioned the importance of upanayana for girls. The Atharvaveda refers to maidens under going the discipline of Brahmacharya.[9]

Participation in Vedic Sacrifices

No sacrifice was complete in which the woman as the spouse of the man performing the sacrifice didn't participate.[10] In Agrahayana ceremony a number of Vedic hymns were recited and the harvest sacrifices were performed by women alone.[11] In the Rámäyana we àlso find Kausalya was performing a sacrifice alone in the morning of her son's proposed installation as a heir-apparent.[12] The same thing happened to Tara when her husband Vali was about to leave the palace to meet Sugreeva in fateful encounter.[13] We can record the instance of Seeta offering her Vedic prayer during the days of her captivity in Lanka.[14] We also find examples from Mahabharat that Kunti was well-versed in the mantras of Atharvavedas.[15]

Centre of Education

During the Vedic period the family played a greater role in the educational system. As professional teachers were not available the father was treated as the usual teacher and the home as the usual school. We find so many examples in Vedic and Upanishadic literature about fathers teaching their sons. Prajapati was the teacher of his son, devas, asuras and men.[16] Aruni had initiated his son Svetaketu in the study of philosophy.[17] We find rare cases of girls being educated at boarding school or colleges. But in Malatimadhava we notice that Kamandaki was educated at a college along with Bhurivasu and Devarata.[18] This is a clear case of sending girls outside for their education. Dharmasutras also point out that the girls should be taught at home by their male guardians like the father, the brother or the uncle.

Co-education

Co-education is not new to our civilization. It was prevalent in Vedic India both boys and girls sitting on the lap of the nature in the so called Tapovans of the forest acquired education in an ideal way from the same Guru. It has been mentioned in the Grihyasutra that the three castes excluding the last one were required to undergo a period of religious studentship. We have also some evidence from Chhandagyopanishada where king Asvapati says that there is no ignorant person in my kingdom.[19] In Uttara Ramacharita, we also find Atreyi receiving education along with Lava and Kusa.[20] So it is clear from the fact that education was not denied to women during Vedic time.

Types of Students

There was no stress of child marriage in that period. Majority of girls used to get married at the age of 16 or seventeen. Only few of them could prosecute their studies after that age. The former classes were called Sadyovadhus and the latter class Brahmavadinis. Along with the study of Vedic hymns and sacrifices, music and dancing were taught to Sadyovadhus. Brahmavadinis used to marry after their education was over. We find in the Ramayana that Vedavati, the daughter of sage Kusadhvaja never got married.[21]

Arrangement for Teaching

Not only the gent teachers but also the lady teachers used to teach the girl students. The gent teachers were called as Upādhyäyas, and the lady teachers as Upädhyaya. Further the wife of a teacher was known as Upadhyayini Panini refers to boarding houses for girl students, Chhatrasalas and these salas were under the supervision of the Upadhyayas or lady teachers.[22] But we do not have any clear evidence of the activities of lady teachers and the management of girls boarding. Girls of rich families must have received good education.

Lady Scholars

During the Vedic period the girls who remained unmarried for longer time, used to have mastery over the Vedic literature. "Lady Students of Katha and Bahvricha School were known as Kathi and Bahvrichi respectively. Kathivrindarika denoted the foremost female student of the Kaths School, indicating the success of some woman students in Vedic branch".[23] Kasakritsnin has composed a treatised on mimamsa. The girls who studied the subject were known as Kasakritsna. Poetesses like Visvavara, Sikata Nivavari, Ghosa, Romasa, Lopamudra, Appala, and Urvasi had composed Vedic hymns. Some distinguished lady scholars like Sulabhã, Vadava, Prithiteyi, Maitreyi and Gargi contributed a lot to the Vedic literature and philosophy. Gargi and Maitreyi took part in philosophical discourse along with the Rishis.

Names of Several South India poetesses like Revi, Roha, Madhavi and Sasiprava were mentioned in the Gatha-Sapta-Sati of Hala.[24]

Education in Cultured Family

The conditions of cultured families were fairly good. The ladies of the royal families achieved a lot in the field of literary education and became good poetesses.[25] They could appoint special teachers for their girls. Special training was given to them in the fields of domestic arts and fine arts like music, painting, and dancing, garland-making and house hold decorations.[26] It has been said in Brihadaranyak upanishada that a parent desirous for birth of a daughter perform rituals. He should pray that his daughter must be a learned one and lived for hundred years.[27]

Education in Ordinary Family

Unlike cultured families, the ordinary families could not employ special teacher for their girls. Literature and fine arts were the subject of study for them. The women took resort to spinning and weaving during their leisure time to help the family and the children.[28]

Women education in Buddhism

Women are allowed to join Sangha. This resulted an indirect impetus to spread women education. Like Brahmavadinis, several ladies became nuns and nunpoetesses to lead a life of celibacy and other went outside India to preach Buddhism. Among the nun-scholars Subha, Anupama, Sumedha, Vijayanka and Sanghamitra were famous. Monastery was the centre of education. Girls from well-to-do families and rich merchants used to get education. Monks and nuns were living separately.

Conclusion

From the above discussions we may conclude the following :

1. Our ancient civilization is unique in respect of the position of women in the society.
2. Education was not denied to women in ancient India.
3. Ladies shared their parts in performing sacrifices along with the gents.
4. Child marriage was not occurred in the society.
5. Most of the educated women engaged themselves with philosophical discourse to know the ultimate reality of life.

6. At last we can create awareness among the people to bring back the past glory of women to the present fold.

REFERENCES

Altekar, A.S., (1975); *Education in Ancient India,* Manohar Prakashan, Varanasi-1.

Dash, B.N., (1994); *Foundation of Educational Thought and Practice,* Kalyani Publishers, New Delhi-2.

Pathak, P.D., (1974); *Bharatiya Shiksha Aur Uski Samasyaen,* Vinod Pustak Mandir, Agra-2.

—, *Chhandagyopanishad,* Geeta Press, Gorakhpur.

—, *Brihadaranyakopanishada,* Geeta Press, Gorakhpur.

—, *Manusmriti,* (1987); Chowkhamba Sanskrit Pratisthan, Delhi-7.

NOTES

1. आलौकिकं पुरूशार्थोपायमं वेत्ति अनेनेति।
2. Education in ancient in India, p. 4
3. ज्ञानं तृतीयं मनुजस्य नेत्रं समस्ततत्वार्थविलोकदक्षः।
   तेजोऽनपेक्षं विगतान्तराय प्रवृत्तिमत्सर्व जगत्त्रयेपि।।
   (सुभाषितरत्नसन्दोहः)
   page 194
4. सा विद्या या विमुक्तये।
5. मातेव रक्षति पितेव हिते नियुक्ते कान्तेव चापि रमयत्यपीयखेदम्।
   लक्ष्मीतनोति वितनोति च दिक्षुकीर्ति किं किं न साधयति कल्पलतेव विद्या।
   (सुभाषितरत्नभाण्डारः), 3.IV.14
6. यत्र नार्यस्तु पूज्यन्ते रमन्ते तत्रदेवताः। (मनुस्मृतिः) पृ. 54
7. आचार्य उपनयमानो ब्रह्मचारिणं कृणुते गर्भमन्तः। (अथर्ववेद–XI)
8. अमन्त्रिका तु कार्येयं स्त्रीणामावृदशेषतः।
   संस्कारार्थे शरीरस्य यथाकालं यथाक्रमम्।। 2/66
9. ब्रह्मचर्येण कन्या युवानं विन्दते पतिम्।
10. अयज्ञिनो वा एष योऽपत्नीकः। शतपथ ब्राह्मण V.1.6.10.
11. पराशरगृह्यसूत्रम् (III.2)
12. सा क्षोभवसना हृष्टा नित्यं व्रत परायणा।
    अग्निं जुहोति स्म तदा मन्त्रा विस्कृतमंगला। II.20.15
13. ततः स्वस्त्ययनं कृत्वा मन्त्रविद्विजयैषिणी। (तत्रैव) (IV-16.12)
14. सन्ध्याकालमनाः श्यामा धृवमेष्यति जानकी।

नदीं चेमां शुभ्रजलां सन्ध्यार्थ वरवर्णिनी। (तत्रैव) (V-15.48)

15. महाभारतम् II.20
16. वृहदारण्यकोपनिषद्। 6.2.1।
17. छान्दोग्योपनिषद्। 5.3.1।
18. अंक–1.
19. V.II.5
20. अंक–2
21. VII.17
22. छात्र्यादयः शालायाम्। VI.2.86
23. A.S. Altekar, Education in Ancient India, page 210.
24. I, II, III & IV
25. काव्यमिमांसा–पृ. 53।
26. कामसूत्रम् 1.3.16।
27. अय य इच्छेद् दुहिता मे जायते सर्वमायुरियादिति तिलौदनं पाचयित्वा सर्पिष्मन्त मश्नीयाताम्। VI.4.17
28. अर्थशास्त्रम् । II/23।

21

POLICIES AND PROGRAMMES ON EDUCATION AND EMPOWERMENT OF WOMEN

—ANIL KUMAR NAIK

Empowerment as a concept was introduced at the International Women's Conference at Nairobi in 1985. The conference defined empowerment as a redistribution of social power and control of resources in favour of women. An important means of women's empowerment is economic independence through information, knowledge and necessary skills. If a woman is economically a versatile parasite, she can never claim an equal status with men. Women's awareness about development is basic to achieving this economic empowerment. Even after half a century of independence, 70% of women workforce is employed and getting paid only in unskilled jobs. (Srivastav, 2005) Women should be provided with upgraded technical skills that alone can ensure a quick beginning of the earnings.

Policies on Education of Women

Let us now review the policies on education of women in India.

National Policy on Education 1986 on Women's Education

The National Policy on Education 1986 was concerned about the status and education of women in the country. The major recommendations were :

"Education will be used as an agent of basic change in the staus of women. In order to neutralize the accumulated disortions of the past there will be a positive, interventionist role in the empowerment of women. Women's studies will be promoted as a part of various courses and educational institutions encouraged to take up active programmes to further women's development. The policy of non-discrimination will be pursued vigorously to eliminate sex-stereo typing in vocational, and professional courses and to promote women's participation in non-traditional occupations, as well as in existing and emergent technologies."

Programme of Action, 1986

The "Programme of Action" has detailed following time-bound targets, policy parameters and strategies for women's education, which are as follows :

(a) A phased, time-bound programme of adult education for women in the age group 15-35 (whose number is estimated to be 6.8 crore) by 1995.

(b) Increased women's access to vocational, technical, professional education and to existing and emergent technologies.

(c) Review and reorganization of the educational activities to ensure that it makes a substantial contribution towards women's equality, and creation of appropriate cells/units therefore.

National Policy on Education Review Committee (NPERC) 1990

The committee reviewed the NPE and POA in the context of women's education and made recommendations with regard to the following dimensions:

- Access to education and equality of learning
- Content of education and gender bias
- Vocational education
- Training of teachers and other educational personnel
- Research and development of women's studies.
- Representation of women in the educational hierarchy
- Employment of women
- Adult education
- Number of women - teachers in co-educational schools should be increased
- Hostel facilities must be made available for girls at all levels.

Programme of Action, 1992

The committee recommended that the following measures will be taken to make the education an effective tool for women's empowerment.

- Enhancing self-esteem and self-confidence of women.

- Enabling women to make informed choice in areas like education, employment and health.
- Providing information, knowledge and skill for economic independence.
- All teachers and instructors will be trained as agents of women's empowerment.
- Special efforts would be made to recruit women teachers and to augment teacher - training facilities for women.

National Policy for the Empowerment of Women 2001

A national policy for the empowerment of women has been announced in 20th March 2001. The origin of the policy lies in the recommendations made in the National Perspective Plan for Women (1988-2000 AD). A commitment to adopt a National Policy for Women was also made in the Fourth World Conference on Women held in Beijing in 1995.

The goal of this policy is to bring about the advancement, development and empowerment of women through a process of change in societal attitudes towards women, elimination of all forms of discrimination against women and active participation of women in all spheres of life, which will empower women both socially and economically.

In the context of adopting human development as the ultimate goal of our development efforts, empowerment of women gains priority on the country's development.

Women, as an independent target group, account for 495.74 million and represent 48.3% of country's total population. Empowering women as a process demands a life cycle approach. Therefore, every stage of their life counts as a priority in the planning process. Women in the economically active age group 15-59 years, who account for 289.40 million (58.4%), have different demands like those of education / training, employment, income generation and participation in the developmental process, decision making etc. (Srivastav, 2005)

Tenth Plan and the Empowerment of Women

In the context of having a laid down National Policy, approach to the tenth plan for empowering women will be very distinct from that of the earlier Plans, as it now stands on a strong platform for Action with definite goals, targets and a time-frame.

To adopt a Sector - specific 3-fold Strategy for empowering

women, based on the prescriptions of National Policy for Empowerment of Women. They include:

Social Empowerment: To create an enabling environment through various affirmative development policies and programmes for development of women besides providing them easy and equal access to all the basic minimum services so as to enable them to realize their full potentials.

Economic Empowerment: To ensure provision of training, employment and income-generation activities with both 'forward' and 'backward' linkages with the ultimate objective of making all potential women economically independent and self-reliant; and

Gender Justice: To eliminate all forms of gender discrimination and thus, allow women to enjoy not only the de-jure but also the de-facto rights and fundamental freedom on par with men in all spheres, viz., political, social, civil, cultural etc.

Different Programmes on Empowerment of Women

Empowerment of women has now become a key issue in the National Development plans. There were many programmes that were taken of by the Government for empowerment of Women. Some of these programme are:

The Swa-Shakti Project: This project was conceptualised by the Department of Women and Child Development. The Project aims at empowerment of women by facilitating a process of social change that would have a positive impact on their life. The project involves in organizing women in Self-Help Groups (SHGs) that work towards gaining access to and control over physical, social, economic resources as well as political process. Bringing women together under Self-Help Groups has resulted in their increasing self-reliance and confidence. The idea behind SHGs is to mobilize women and improve their quality of life.

Women's Economic Programme: This programme was launched in 1982 with asistance from the Norwegian Agency for Development Corporation, (NORAD). Under this programme, financial assistance is given to the Women Development corporations, autonomous bodies and voluntary organizations to train poor women mostly in non-traditional areas to ensure their employment in these areas.

Training women and providing them technical support improves their skills heading to productivity. The aim is to bring in more income in the hands of women so that they can lead a better social life.

Support to Training and Employment Programme of women: It was launched in 1987 to provide new knowledge and update skills of poor and assetless women in the traditional sectors such as Agriculture, Animal Husbandry, Dairying, Fisheries, Handloom, Handicrafts, Khadi and Village Industries, Sericulture, Social Forestry and waste land Development for enhancing their productivity and incomes.

Support Services for Women: The Scheme for support services for Women, Balika Samridhi Yojana was launched in 1997 with the aims to change the community's attitude towards the girls. The mother of a girl child born after August 15, 1997 in a family beolw poverty line is given a grant of Rs. 500 to be deposited in an interest bearing account of a financial Institution in the name of girl child. In addition the girl child will become eligible to annual scholarships for each successfully completed year of schooling.

Hostel for Working Women: The Department of Women and Child Development are implementing the Scheme of construction/ expansion of Hostel Building for Working Women with a Dairy Care Centre. The objective of the scheme is to provide hostel accommodation at moderate rates to enable women to seek employment or participate in Technical Training.

Short stay Homes for Women and Girls: The short stay homes for women and girls were started in 1969 to protect and rehabilitate those girls or women who face moral danger, mental strain, and social ostracism due to family problems.

Rehabilitation of Marginalised Women: The Government also started scheme for rehabilitation of marginalized women for providing shelter, medical facilities, pensions and security to the widows.

Education of Women: Commensurate with the worldwide emerging demand for empowerment of women, India recognized that women education has become pertinent. It has become the critical precondition for empowerment of women. In order to give a focused attention to accelerate women literacy particularly among the socially and economically weaker section of society, who are debarred from and are devoid of learning for various reasons. The Government of India had taken recourse to comprehensive literacy drive for women.

Several adult education programmes have been initiated in the country. Some of these are:

1. Social Education (started in 1951)
2. Farmer's Functional Literacy Programme (in 1967)
3. Non-Formal Education (in 1978)
4. National Literacy Mission (in 1988)
5. Total Literacy Campaign (in 1991)

Considering the grave situation of continued victimization of women and girl children and the critical needs of education in life, the Government of India has implemented various policy measures to promote and accelerate women's education in India, including education of girl child on a holistic approach both at the Central and State levels. To expedite women literacy ratio as well as to reduce school dropout rates substantially for which several incentive schemes have been adopted like Sarva Shiksha Abhiyan, Mahila Samakhya, Mid-day Meal Scheme etc.

Sarva Shiksha Abhiyan (SSA)

The Sarva Shiksha Abhiyan is a comprehensive scheme launched in the year 2000 in joint collaboration with the State with an objective of widening the scope of elementary education through out the country. This scheme seeks to bridge gender inequality by giving due emphasis to promote education of girl child in the society and on a larger scale to afford them social justice, security and equity at par with the boy child. The programme aims to improve the performance of school system through community owned approach and to impart qualitative elementary education to all children in the age group of 6 to 14 years by 2010.

Under this scheme, the National Programme Nutritional Support to Primary Education (Mid-day Meal Scheme) and National Programme for Education of Girls at Elementary Level (NPEGEL) were implemented to provide additional support to education of girls at the elementary level.

Adult Education Programme

With a view to achieve education for all by 2000 AD, the National Literacy Mission came up with different plans and srategies. Most important among them is to make this programme a people's programme and cover women, the important resource of the society. The specific objectives of adult education programme are :

Achieving self-reliance in literacy and numeracy.

- Becoming aware of the causes of deprivation and moving towards the amelioration of those oppressive conditions through organized participation in the process of development.
- Acquiring the skills necessary for improving the economic status and well being of women.
- Imbibing the value of women's equality and empowerment.

Conclusion

The success of these programmes also requires reviews of national development plans as well as the regular policy, planning and implementation cycles of different ministries. However, mechanisms need to be developed with capacity, commitment and political backing to champion change across different institutions. While different programmes for empowerment of women are mainly the concerned and always start with the Government for achieving the outcome, some of these programmes can be extended to other kinds of organizations as well.

Women's participation in higher education has been improved and considerable progress has been made. A lot needs to be done. We should adopt strategy for empowering women based on the prescription of the national policy for empowerment of women. They include social empowerment, economic empowerment and gender justice.

REFERENCES

Begum, (2006), *Women Entrepreneurship in India, Challenges and Strategies*, University News, 44 (15), April 10-16.

Government of India, (1986), *National Poilcy On Education.* New Delhi: MH.R.D.

Government of India, (1990), *N.P.E. R. C. - 1990*, New Delhi: MH.R.D.

Government of India, (1992), *Revised Policy Formulations of N.P.E. 1986,* New Delhi: MH.R.D.

Government of India, (2001), *National Policy For Empowerment of Women,* New Delhi: D. W. C. D.

Pandian, C., (2006), *Role of Universities in Empowering Weaker Sections of the Society,* University News, 44(16), April 17-23.

Srivastava, G., (2006), *Women's Identity in the Indian Society: Educational Perspective,* University News, 44 (24) June, 12-18.

22

WOMEN EDUCATION —Emerging Issues and Remedies

—SIDHARTH SHANKAR RATH

Introduction

The condition of present day society reminds me of a painting by a world-renowned spanish artist slavadore Dali. The canvas had a world in its centre on one side half of the world was in a shadow. The other half was in sunlight. Half of the world in shadow to the left revealed a shrunken image, a midget walking away from the world in the black tunnels of despair towards the blackangel of destruction waiting for him/her. To the right was the world of sunlight the persons self-image was tall, walking towards the dawn of accomplishment witth a shallow flying to-words the sun. To the left in the world of darkness was an individual on a ship about to be capsized flowndexing on rough seas of negative feelings. To the right in the world of sunlight, the person in a ship was moving in calm waters towards a port, towards a goal. This is the condition of the present day society. Half of the world in the darkness is full of frustration and destruction and half of the world in the sunlight is with confidence and faith.

Problems of the Day

In the world today the problems we are witnessing are erosion of moral values. Girls moving half naked in the streets with half a dozen boy friends, attending bars, hotels, taking alcohols or drugs and coming home late night, paying no respect to elders. This picture we now see in some of the highly educated city breed families. There is cessasion of family responsibilities, highly educated women in high positions do not want to bear child in their wombs. Even some of the women are unwilling for breast feeding. Some of the employed women do not desire to spend their earning for the wholesale development of the family and demand for separation from the rest of the family members. There is selfish and autocratic nature in women. They are becoming very selfish and self centered. Behaving like autocrats as if they have no sympathy or kindness to others. There is emergence of many social evils like divorce, broken conjugal life rape, molestation child pregnancy, pre-marital sex etc. The number is more among the educated classes and elites. Loss of faith in native culture, tradition, social and religious occasions is seen. Although we are observing increasing tendency in respect of festivity among the educated city people, their number is more in religious assemblies and festivals. But this is to enhance their social status in the eyes of others. They observe the festivals as a source of entertainment not for their own spiritual development. There is maintenance of materialistic life style. Love for materialism is a sign of civilization. Maintaining an easy comfortable life. No respect for labour.

These are some of the negative aspects of our time.

The Necessity of the day

Education should spread among the girls. Women should be empowered and liberated. They should be independent but not autocrats. We expect to see so many Seetas, Sabitris, Anusuyas, Gandharies because the society needs them for development, restoration of moral values, revival of culture etc. but we are harassed to see so many Mantharas, Surpanekhas, Dianas and Malikas in the society. It is a matter of great regret that the younger generation of girls do not take Seeta or Sabitri or Laxmibai as their role models to imitate rather, Malika, Diana, Bipasa as their gurus and copy their life in films in the copy book style. This is a fact and we must admit it. We witness the absence of true mother in our society. So how could a society be made?

Again it is said that women should come out of their kitchen and share a larger burden of the society. They should contribute for social prosperity and to make their presence in the decision making table in our parliament. More members in the offices and parliaments means more concessions to women in every respect. The sorry state of affairs which I cited above are not due to the spread of education only rather the causes are invasion of western culture cable TV (the Idiot box) globalisation and our infatuation maintain a western type of life style. Talibanisation of India is not desirable. Indian women look beautiful with sarees and vermilion rather in Biknis, lingeries and swim suits. Hence it is certain that this is due to the impact of education to some extent. If a woman looks like a mother in dress and behaviour, no doubt she will be worshipped as mother.

Remedies for the ills

There is no remedy or medicine to change human mind which is mad after money, sex and luxury. But we should not be pessimistic. The ground must be prepared.

1. Introduction of value based education from primary schools. A value based education is the foundation for every childs development. Education should bring the confidence of the student at the secondary level. It must create an atmosphere where every student will feel pride in their own culture.
2. Introduction of curriculum that integrates universal values and character development should be made.
3. Study and visit to holy places of worship of different religions are to be undertaken.
4. Emphasis on diversity as an asset be made.
5. Development of early exposure and love for culture, religions and traditions should be made.
6. Early exposure and love for diverse languages be made.
7. There should be school to school and college to college exchanges.
8. There should be commitment and equal emphasis on the education of both sexes providing equal opportunities and facilities to all at the school.
9. There should be promotion of co-operative games, consultation and collaboration between diverse student bodies.
10. Debates should be organised to create a support base for cultural marvels among students.
11. Children should be exposed to culture to learn to cherish it.
12. Parents, teachers and students should do service camps together.

Conclusion

Humanity is going through a major transformation from the state of childhood to maturity from disintegrated nations to a global society.

Education in order to be holistic and to be able to meet the needs of our time should ensure a balanced development of physicaı, intellectual and spiritual dimensions of life. Moral education is an integral part of every educational activity and it must be included in educational activity and it must be included in educational curriculum at schools. In the age of globalisation we must stand with our heads high with our distinct cultural identity.

WOMEN EDUCATION —Emerging Issues and Rethinking

—Padmalaya Panda

Education moulds the destiny of a nation in which women play a prominent role in the society. Women and men are two sides of a coin. Women perform multifarious roles, i.e., mother, sister, wife, friend, guide and in many cases as wage earners. According to Manu, "Yatra Naryante Pujyate Prianta Tasya Devta". God becomes satisfied where there is great respect for women. She is the creator; well-wisher for the society and in some cases takes the form of Mother Durga to abolish injustice, evil and establishes Truth and Justice. Thus women education is a challenging issue in our society. Great warrior Napoleon rightly remarked, "Give me an educated mother, I shall promise you the birth of a civilized nation". According to Vedas, Smrities and Convention, a wife is the half of the husband and shares his merits and demerits. The teacher and the father have always been the objects of worship but the mother is considered as far superior to them. The mother who is inquiring and alert, well informed and familiar with subjects such as history and literature, who lives and works with her children in the home will be the best teacher in the world of both character and intelligence. History of India proves that the woman occupies the position of the key stone in the arch of Hindu Social Structure. Women have become equal partners with the men in all religious and social duties. But gradually with the introduction of early marriage and blind belief there was change in co-education. During Muslim period women's condition rotted behind the pardah and they were deprived of education. During British regime from the Bethune's period women education slightly improved. With the effort of Hunter, Annie Besant, Margaret, women's position became better. Mahatma Gandhi, Raja Ram Mohan Roy contributed a lot for the development of women's education.

Education and Women's Equality

Provision of education opportunities to women has been an important programme in education since independence which promotes national integration and functions the democratic order properly. Indian Constitution in Article 16 imposed non-discrimination on ground of sex in public employment and Article 15(3) empowered the state to make special provision for the welfare and development of women and children which justify special allocation and relaxation of procedures & conditions to expand a girl's access to education at different levels. The N.P.E., 1986 regarding education for women's equality, states — "education will be used as an agent of basic change in the status of women". To analyse equalization of women's opportunities following 10 dimensions are taken into consideration.

1. Access to education and quality learning.
2. Content of education and gender bias.
3. Vocational equation for women.
4. Training of teachers & other personnel.
5. Research and Development in women's studies.
6. Representation of women in educational hierarchy.
7. Empowerment of women.
8. Adult women education.
9. Resources.
10. Management.

1. Access to Education and Quality Learning: To analyse "Access to education and quality learning" following four factors are taken into consideration. They are :

(a) Water, fuel and fodder

(b) ECCE (Early childhood care and education)

(c) Availability of schooling

(d) Regional disparities.

***(a) Water, Fuel and Fodder*:** In remote rural places women and girl children are given the responsibility of collecting water, fuels and fodder for their family. So they are unable to attend the school. Therefore it is necessary to make water, fuel and fodder easily accessible on a priority basis to those habitation and communities whose enrolment and retention rates for girls in schools are below the state average.

(b) ECCE: The impact on ECCE's child centred approach in the learning at schools should be strengthened. The girl children of age 0-6 should be prepared for the school. Older girls should be relieved from sibling care to attend school. It is also necessary to allow the women teachers to avail day care facilities for their children and attend school regularly.

Moreover, the ECCE Centres should be located near primary school and their training should be included in school hours. The teacher training and curriculum should be redesigned from Class I to III to incorporate with ECCE approaches. There should be co-ordination between Anganwadi workers and social teachers.

(c) Availability of Schooling: It can be studied under following points :

(i) Primary School: The official norm of 1 KM walking distance for providing primary school is not sufficient. Primary schools should be provided with 300 population and should be inter-linked with para schools to co-ordinate with other primary schools in the inserved habitations.

(ii) Middle School: The official norm of 3 KM walking distance is also not sufficient. Middle school should be provided with a population of 500 and are to be linked with para middle school in the inserved area.

(iii) Non-formalizing the School: Making the formal school less rigid, Involvement of village committees formalizing the school. In this context the local needs will have to be identified. The educational complex and the village educational committees will be in the best position to organize school work. Para teachers (Siksha Karmi) should be recruited from the locality to work efficiently.

(iv) Other measures to attract girls to schools: Girls engaged in wage labour should be given incentives like scholarship, free uniform, text books etc. to make them able to attend the school.

(v) Secondary and Higher secondary schools: Better transport facilities should be provided for girls. Number of girls' schools should be opened with residential facility at minimum cost and free for S.T. and S.C. children.

(vi) Higher Education: Opportunities should be increased for the women to pursue higher studies besides traditional courses like

medicine, veterinary science, engineering, law etc. by providing hostel facilities and scholarships, free text books and relaxation of age limit etc.

(d) Regional Disparities: Regional disparities are observed at state, districts and block levels which are not encountered by decentralized and participative mode of planning and management.

2. Content of Education and Gender Bias: The curriculum is stereotype in text book and hidden and the role of the media.

The N.C.E.R.T. women's cell is responsible for the component of core-curriculum relating to women's equality by increasing visibility of women in history, epics etc. and to provide the basic legal information including the protective laws regarding women and make them aware of the fundamental rights.

The text books prepared by N.C.E.R.T., S.C.E.R.T. and other publishers should be reviewed to eliminate the invisibility of women and the gender stereotype, hidden curriculum etc. and for proper incorporation of women in teaching of all subjects. The powerful role in reflecting and perpetuating dominant social value in area of gender in equality is well known.

3. Vocational Education for Women: In practice it is seen that options for scientific and technical professional courses are rarely available to the women. Therefore diversification of courses and grades to match with the job potential of women at local levels may be implemented.

For encouraging access to technical or crafts the Training institutions should increase stipend, fellowships and a system of placement cell be made available. There should be at least one women's polytechnic in each district.

4. Training of Teachers and Other Personnel: The teachers training programme is a centralized activity of N.C.E.R.T., women's cell, N.I.E.P.A. (National Institute of Educational Planning and Administration), U.G'.C. etc. which includes sensitivity to women's problem, decentralization of curriculum planning and implementation. Also in-service training programmes may be organized by D.I.E.T. and Educational complexes.

5. Research and Development in Women's Studies: Research can be a major input in incorporating women's issues perspectiveness and concern at all stages of education create a concrete input in all areas of curricular development and training of teachers.

6. Representation of Women in Educational Hierarchy: Women should be recruited at a different level of education. There should be promotion in educational hierarchy. They should represent in decision making, in teaching and educational administration, in selection and departmental promotion committees.

7. Empowerment of Women: Mahila Samakhya should be developed in a decentralized and participative mode of management with the decision making power at district and block level and ultimately for poor women in group. It should be implemented to establish organic linkages with E.C.C.E. programmes and efforts may be made towards universalisàtion of women's education along with the means of economic independence for women. Issues of women's health including reproductive health should be implemented in the parameters for empowerment of women.

8. Adult Women Education: For imparting adult women education and thereby empowering them, the Mahila Samakhya model should be tried out.

9. Resources: To give a well conceived edge to education in favour of women it requires a significant increase in allocation of resources in plan and non-plan sectors.

10. Management: The responsibility for planning implementing and internal monitoring of all school programmes for women's education should be handed over to educational complexes in the Panchayat Raj frame work. At the institutional level, the Heads of the institutions should be made fully responsible for micro level planning and ensuring universalisation of girls education and their access to high school vocational education according to disaggregated strategies and time frame.

The national education system will play a positive interventionist role in the empowerment of women. It will foster the development of new values through well-designed curriculum, text book training, orientation of teachers, decision makers and administrators and active involvement of educational institutions. Change in the attitude of the public towards women education would go a long way in improving the situation. Major emphasis should be given on women's participation in vocation, technical and professional at different levels.

REFERENCES

J.C. Aggarwal, *Modern Trends in Indian Education*.

Mohanty J. *Modern Trend in Indian Education.*

Reddy S., *N.P.E. 1986 In the emerging Indian Society.*

—, N.P.E. 1986, N.C.E.R.T.

WOMEN EDUCATION —Issues and Approaches

—K.P. NAYAK AND DILLIP KUMAR NAYAK

Introduction

A woman influences every member 'of the family in varieties of roles that she plays. There was a time when a woman's place was in the kitchen and a man's in the farm, factory or office. In many parts of the world this is no longer true. Women look after families and make better homes, but today they also occupy the highest offices in several countries. Women now play almost all the games and enjoy nearly every sports that men do. Let us look back and introspect.

Retrospective View

After independence, the Constitutional guarantee of equality changed the conceptual thinking of educational development of women and gave a call to women to play multiple roles in the polity, economy and society. The educational development of women began in that broad direction. This is amply evident in the Government's policy, reports of various committees and commissions set up for this purpose and in the objectives of Development Plans formulated after Independence. The National Policy of Education provides that "The Education of girls should receive emphasis not only on grounds of social justice but also because it accelerates social transformation". The very First Five Year Plan stated, "The general purpose and objective of Women's education cannot, of course, be different from the purpose and objectives of the men's education. At the Secondary and even at the University stage women's education should have a vocational or occupational bias". Similarly, the Secondary Education Commission (1953) stated that "In a democratic society where all citizens have to discharge their civic and social obligations, differences, which may lead to variations in the standard of intellectual development achieved by boys and girls can be envisaged". The Report of the Committee on Differentiation of Curricula for boys and girls (1959) also emphasised on the same type of education and same role of men and women in the society. The Education Commission (1964-66) endorsed the recommendations of all committees and commissions about the equality in the educational development of women. The Government's national policy also laid down that "The education system must produce young men and women of character and ability committed to national services and development. Only then education will be able to play its vital role in promoting national progress, creating a sense of common citizenship and culture strengthening national integration."

In spite of the constitutional provision of equality and the recommendations of the committees and commissions the provision for the same type of education for women as for men has become limited. The view point of women's education, with a separate role of women in the society has had a great influence on the planning for women's education.

Women are clearly at a dis advantage stage in India, with regard to education. Literacy figures give clear picture of the educational status of Indian girls and women. The 1991 census data indicate that only 39% of females above age seven are literate, as opposed to 64% of males. Of the 324 million illiterates enumerated in India in 1991, 197 million (61%). were girls and women (World Bank 1996:52). The 2001 Census revealed that 65.4% people (75.85 among men and 54.16 among women) are now literate, and that for the first time the absolute number of illiterates actually went down.

More than two million women have been enrolled for higher education in India today. The figure may sound impressive to those who are not fully aware of the size of the population of the country. However, these 2 million women constitute just 34% of the total enrolment of 6.5 million students in higher education. It is interesting that the percentage of women is slightly higher at the post-graduate level (39%) than at the under-graduate level (34%), and this is higher at this level than the enrolment in the diploma level (26%). Data, on the faculty-wise distribution of women, shows that of all the women enrolled in higher education, 54% are enrolled in Arts and Humanities, 20% are enrolled in Science, 14% in Commerce, 4% in Medicine, Agriculture and Management, 2% in law and 1% in

Engineering.

Issues

There are several factors that contribute to the problems of women education in India. The factors are as follows :

- Poor economic and social status of parents particularly in unorganized and informal sectors and slums pressurizing young girls to earn at an early stage in
  - (i) Agricultural occupations,
  - (ii) Homebased industry-carpet weaving, and beedi rolling,
  - (iii) Assisting mothers by working as domestic help in middle class homes
  - (iv) Selling incense sticks, domestic materials etc. and
  - (v) Taking care of siblings at home.
- Non-availability of colleges, insufficient budgetary allocations and non-availability of basic physical facilities (lack of adequate facilities like, toilets, commonrooms, hostels etc.).
- Introduction of inappropriate subjects and disciplines in curriculum
- Non-availability of scholarships/fellowships and disciplines of their choice.
- Absence of women teachers, separate schools and colleges for women and safety measures
- Absence of counselling for discipline and career options, role model etc.
- Gender stereotyping in course content, subject choice and gender disparity
- Restrictive practices, conservative attitudes and violence against women
- Discriminatory attitudes of teachers and administrators
- Education being perceived as un-productive and irrelevant for development.

Approaches and Methods

The world has realised these days that women's education requires greater attention than it received in the past. In most large cities and towns in our country, there are now special schools for girls. In addition to these there are many co-educational schools where girls and boys study together. Most parents now allow their daughters to attend co-educational schools, though there are some parents who are against such schools for girls after the age of 11 or 12. A large percentage of women now go to college to pursue graduate, postgraduate and professional studies. Medicine and teaching in particular attract a growing number of talented girls. In spite of all this, however, women's education is still lagging behind and requires much greater attention. The government must encourage the opening of new schools for girls and grant more scholarships to women students who do well in studies or who come from poor families.

Following measures need attention in improving women education :

- Conservative attitude of the society towards women should be changed.
- Increasing the educational facilities and opportunities for women.
- Removal of traditional bars on entry of women to particular branches, occupations and levels of education.
- Their capabilities should be fully developed, utilized and recognized.
- Involvement of women, both as paid functionaries and as volunteers, at different levels in community development programmes should be made.
- There should be abolition of discrimination against women through the empowerment of women by laws.
- The workshop-format should be used, and learners should be urged to participate actively in the group activities.
- Care should be exercised to incorporate the diverse individual experiences of the learners who come from a variety of backgrounds in the teaching learning process.
- Putting learning experience into practice, through the use of artistic forms of creation or opinions, the achievement of financial independence, active participation in the decision-making process, and networking.
- Encouraging research on issues related to women's status and role.
- Elimination of sexist bias and sex stereotypes from textbooks.

- Advancing knowledge by expanding the information base with the help of application of information technology.
- Dissemination of information and interaction through seminars/ workshops on the need for Women's Studies and its role in University education.
- Orientation of teachers and researchers to handle women-related topics and to incorporate women's dimension into general topics.

Conclusion

Families rely on mothers and wives for emotional support and care; families rely on women for labour in the home; and increasingly, families rely on women for income needed to raise healthy children and care for other relatives.It is true that if women are healthy and educated, their families will flourish. If women are free from violence, their families will flourish. If women have a chance to work and earn as full and equal partners in society, their families will flourish. And when families flourish, communities and nations will flourish. That is why every woman, every man, every child, every family, and every nation on our planet has a stake in the struggle for gender equality. Now it is time to act on behalf of women everywhere. If we take bold steps to better the lives of women, we will be taking bold steps to better the lives of children and families too. Now it is the time for us to stand up for the cause of women. It is for men to get out of their system of convenience and supremacy to stand for the cause of women in particular. Let every women to get the chance she deserves to realize her God-given potential.

- Advancing knowledge by expanding the information base with the help of applications of information technology.
- Dissemination of information and interaction through seminars and workshops on the need for Women's Studies and its role in University education.
- Orientation of teachers and researchers to handle women-related topics and to incorporate women's dimension into general topics.

Conclusion

Families rely on mothers and wives for emotional support and care, families rely on women for labour in the home, and increasingly families rely on women for income needed to raise healthy children and care for other relatives. It is true that if women are healthy and educated, their families will flourish. If women are free from violence, their families will flourish. If women have a chance to work and earn as full and equal partners in society, their families will flourish. And when families flourish, communities and nations will flourish. That is why every woman, every man, every child, every family and every nation on our planet has a stake in the struggle for gender equality. Now it is time to act on behalf of women everywhere. If we take bold steps to better the lives of women, we will be taking bold steps to better the lives of children and families too. Now it is the time for us to stand up for the cause of women. It is the time to get out of their system of convenience and supremacy to stand for the cause of women in particular. Let every women to get the dignity she deserves to realize her God-given potential.

25

WOMEN EDUCATION IN THE KBK REGION OF ORISSA —Status and Threats

—MAHESWAR PANDA

The Status

KBK region of Orissa covering the undivided districts of Kalahandi, Bolangir and Koraput have since 1992-93 been divided into 8 districts, viz., Kalahandi, Nuapada. Bolangir, Sonepur, Koraput, Malkangiri, Nawarangpur and Rayagada. The percentage of people below the poverty line (BPL) in these 8 districts being 62.71, 85.70, 61.06, 73.02. 83.81, 81.88, 73.66 and 72.03 respectively indicates the economic backwardness of the people concerned (Table-25.2). The region covering these districts, has, therefore been reported as one of' the most backward regions of the country. All the districts in the region excepting Sonepur are below the state literacy of 63.61 per cent. The women literacy rate in these districts also being 29.56%, 26.01%, 39.27%, 47.28%, 24.81%, 21.28%, 21.02% and 24.31% respectively compares unfavourably with the state average of 50.97 % as well as national average of 54.16%. An observation of the data given in Table-25.1 reveals that the gap in men and women literacy rates in most of these districts is more than the national gap of' 21.69% as well as state gap of 24.98%. Further, the data in the said Table exhibit a deplorable condition of women literacy in the region since the women literacy rate in most of these districts (except Bolangir and Sonepur) is nearly 50% or less than 50% of' the men literates. Besides, an analysis of the figures in Table 25.2 clearly establishes the fact that there exists'an inverse relationship between percentage of women literacy and percentage of population below poverty line (BPL) and thereby suggests enhancing women literacy to improve the economic standard of the people living in the region. The existing scenario of women education in the KBK region therefore, draws special attention of all concerned.

Several educational initiatives in the post-independent era have been taken with a view to give a boost to this spread of education in the area. The programmes and schemes like Operational Black Board (OB). District Primary Education Programme (DPEP), TLP, PLP, Mid-Day Meals (MDM), Educational Guarantee Schemes (EGS), Alternative Innovative Education, Sarva Sikshya Abhiyan (SSA), Janashala, Balika Samridhi Yojana, Mahila Samridhi Yojana, Integrated Child Developed Scheme (ICDS). Early Childhood Care Education (ECCE). Mahila Samakshya (education for women's equality), distribution of free uniforms, etc. have however, proved little effective for the improvenment of women education in the KBK region due to a number of reasons.

The Major Threats

It is desirable here to focus on the major threats that stand on the way of achieving satisfactory improvement in respect of women education in the region.

- Poverty, conservatism, superstitions, ambivalent attitude of parents and communities towards women education coupled with assumption of domestic responsibilities propel the girl children out of formal education.
- The system of child marriage, child labour and polygamy prevalent in this tribal dominated region debar girls from getting education.
- High rate of drop out along with lack of communication/ transportation, infrastructural facilities, girls' schools as well as lack of suitable teaching learning materials for tribal and regional language speaking people are some pertinent hindrances.
- Above all, lack of adequate involvement of educational institutions, community and NGOs at the grass root level and lack of post-literacy follow-up hamper women education in this region.

The Endnote

Needless to state that the status of women education in the KBK region is very discouraging. The education of women in the region should therefore, receive greater emphasis than ever before so as

Table 25.1 : Literacy Rate (per cent) by Sex in KBK Districts of Orissa

Sl. No.	*District*	*Sex*		*Total*	*Gap in Men & Women Literacy*
		Men	*Women*		
1.	Kalahandi	62.88	29.56	46.20	33.32
2.	Nuapada	58.78	26.01	42.29	36.77
3.	Bolangir	70.36	39.27	54.93	31.09
4.	Sonepur	80.30	47.28	64.07	33.02
5.	Koraput	47.58	24.81	36.20	22.77
6.	Malkagiri	41.21	21.28	31.26	19.93
7.	Nawarangpur	47.37	21.02	34.26	26.35
8.	Rayagada	47.35	24.31	35:61	23.04
	Orissa	75.95	50.97	63.61	24.98
	India	75.85	54.16	65.38	21.69

Table 25.2 : Women Literacy and Population Below Poverty Line in KBK Districts

Sl. No.	*Districts*	*% of Women Literacy*	*% of BPL (1997)*
1.	Kalahandi	29.56	62.71
2.	Nuapada	26.01	85.70
3.	Bolangir	39.27	61.06
4.	Sonepur	47.28	73.02
5.	Koraput	24.81	83.81
6.	Malkangiri	21.28	81.88
7.	Nwarangpur	21.02	73.66
8.	Rayagada	24.31	72.03

Source: Department of School & Mass Education, Govt. of Orissa (2003): Vision-2020.

to empower them to fight against hunger, poverty, ignorance and ill-health which are considered as the formidable problems of the people of the region. And if we really expect the women to contribute substantially in building of a healthy and prosperous nation, education is the only answer..

REFERENCES

Department of School and Mass Education, Government of Orissa (2003) : *Vision 2020: An Agenda for School and Mass Education*-Report of the Task Force.

Kochhar, S.K., (2000), *Pivotal Issues in Indian Education,* Sterling Publishers Pvt. Ltd., New Delhi, India.

Mahapatra, P. C., (2003), *Universal Literacy and Empowerment,* Cited in Vision 2020 : An Agenda for School and Mass Education, Government of Orissa. pp. 108-09.

UNICEF, (2005), *A World Fit for Children,* New York, USA, pp. 7-8.

Usha, K., (2003), *Gender Equality and Development,* Yojana, Ministry of Information and Broadcasting, Government of India, Vol. 47, No. 3, pp. 8-9.

26

WOMEN EDUCATION UNDER VEIL OF CONSERVATISM

—Sadananda Mishra

A girl child is often born discriminated and she is further discriminated in the chains of society by everybody from a parent to a parliamentarian. Discrimination is born out of conservatism—age old social prejudices, and traditional mindset of elders, moreover the 'male ego', in various identities. Indeed, no girl child is born weak or feeble, illiterate, unemployed, raped, divorced and the like. She is rather pushed to be so in the slow poisoning process of discrimination, deliberate or otherwise, of our society. In consequence she becomes a baby unwanted, if not then simply compromised; a daughter under nourished; a sister underrated; a peer/class mate harassed; a grownup felt burden; a bride tortured; a wife dominated and an old aged neglected.

In other words, conservatism is the root behind all our setbacks in promoting women education and their status in society. It always restricts a woman from any activity of her will and interest. She is even denied to certain necessities. Can we remove it, although deep rooted from ages, in our mindset? If 'yes', then prevailing discrimination shall automatically cease and any woman can independently rise at par. Thus it needs a societal revolution from bottom than any governmental reformation from the top since, there is no dearth to Policies, Acts, Programmes or Schemes in our country in order to protect the rights of women and promote their education and status in society. Still our achievement always remains poor. Despite of lot of initiatives at various levels, international/national/state the signs of women backwardness are no less visible.

Suggestions

Client's Readiness: It is important. We can help but cannot continue to help some body unless the latter seeks claims or help. So it is far more important to make her ready to seek help than to help her always. So a system whatever decentralized and benevolent it may be cannot possibly afford to ask each of its clients to seek any help or assume certain right that to in every field from home to work place. So we'll have to promote readiness in each of our girl child from her infancy better early than never, breaking all our conservative mindset and beyond 'male ego'.

Prioritizing Areas of Services: What a Girl child really needs in order to rise at par in the society are to be identified. She really needs Care, Education, Income and Security. So more attention and necessary effort are required to ensure all this to every girl child.

Parents Education: Women education should be coupled with parents education. especially the education of mothers. It must help remove all sorts of conservative attitude of parents and society towards girls.

Contents of Women Education: More attention should be given to the study of the following essential aspects: Functional Literacy, Moral education, Physical education including marital art, Home Science Vocational training, legal education, education of health and hygiene.

Operating Vocational Girls' Schools: Such schools are to be opened in vulnerable areas in order to educate girls with different vocations suitable to the girls concerned areas.

Concentrating Vulnerable Groups: More attention is to be given to the vulnerable groups: Rural dwellers, urban slum dwellers, tribes, pavement dwellers, prisoners, construction workers, sex workers child labourers, broken-home victims-Orphans, divorcees, rape victims, handicapped, poverty stricken and the disadvantaged. They constitute majority of women population.

Building Sense of Optimism in Girls. Feeling of despair and cynicism is to be changed to confidence and trust. Once a girl realizes that she can know she must craze to learn.

Reverse Role Playing by Counterparts: Beyond male ego every father/brother/boy at school or college/groom/husband and leader of community and state in his socio-professional life is expected to play reverse, not simply to share. It should begin at home or family. If a brother can clean house and clothes for his sister, a husband can cook for his wife and a father can nurse the baby then all our male ego will die down gradually. This preparedness is required among all male counterparts.

Fixing Accountability: Specific accountability is to be fixed on Panchayats. All developmental works should be provided to a Panchayat subject to its performance in women education.

Leading Role of Educated Women: It is often found that women are the victims of women. So the educated women are supposed to take the lead of the revolution against neglect of women first from each family.

No Competition against Counterpart: Women should not try to compete with men in order to beat them at their own games. Women should rather try to rise to their own ambition. Then only a new civilization can come which is based on love and compassion not on competition or rivalry. This would believe in living together.

The ultimate submission is,—"If we are honestly interested in promoting women education and their status in society, then no longer there should be any game of chase and escape. Let's initiate a revolution in all our mind and action and break all sorts of conservatism around a woman."

EMPOWERING WOMEN THROUGH EDUCATION —Building Bridges for Future

—NARENDRA KUMAR RANA

Prelude

In the words of our Hon'ble President A.P.J. Abdul Kalam "Empowering women is a pre-requisite for creating a good nation, when women are empowered, society with stability is assured. Empowerment of women is essential as their thoughts and value systems lead the development of good family, good society and ultimately a good nation", Women play a significant role in the education of family and thereby promoting sustainable development of the county. Peace, prosperity and stability of a family depend on the education of the females who formulate household budget in a manner that it builds up the healthy family environment. The family budget is oriented towards the provision of qualitative education and health facilities to the children so that they become competitive and promote cohesive social and economic development benefiting all the sections in the country. It is also a well known fact that the education of a girl is the education of the family continuing its impact on the future generations. The involvement of a woman in the decision making process at different layers of the government and private bodies is highly conducive to the overall welfare of the people and of all of the developmental activities. So educating a woman is the cornerstone for empowering her.

Dimensions of Women Empowerment

Empowerment is a multi-dimensional social process that helps people gain control over their lives communities and society by acting on important issues. Empowerment of women involves economic opportunities, property rights, political representation, social equality, personal rights, self-governance, self-sufficiency and self-maintenance. But, women most of the time, are even deprived of some of the fundamental human rights and this denial is justified often in the name of tradition. But the national policy of empowerment of women has set certain clear-cut goals and objectives.

The goal of this policy is to bring about the advancement and empowerment of women. Specifically the objectives of this policy include—

- Creating an environment through positive economic and social policies for full development of women to enable them to realize their full potential.
- The de-jure and de-facto enjoyment of all human rights and fundamental freedom by women on equal basis with men in all spheres — political, economic, social, cultural and civil.
- Equal access for participation and decision making of women in different spheres.
- Equal access of women for healthcare, quality education at all levels, career and vocational guidance, employment, equal remuneration, occupational health and safety, social security and public office etc.
- Strengthening legal systems aimed at elimination of all forms of discrimination against women.
- Changing societal attitudes and community practices by active participation and involvement of both men and women.
- Main streaming a gender perspective in the development process.
- Elimination of discrimination and all forms of violence against women and girl child, and
- Building and strengthening partnerships with civil society, particularly women's organization.

Women's Education as Basis for Women Empowerment

Although education is essential for everyone but incase of women it is particularly significant. Education not only opens up vast avenues and opportunities for growth but affects families and future generations as well. It is, therefore, realized that women have to be provided with the vital educational inputs, if they are to become a powerful force in the society and gain a foot hold in the developmental process. So, giving education to women will reduce their dependency and enhance their status. It will also-

- reduce fertility and slow population growth,
- improve child survival,
- increase the share of family income allocated to food and health care for children.
- raise household income, especially in families below the poverty line and ensure gender equality etc.

The policy of the Government of India for empowerment and development of women lays emphasis on removal of women's illiteracy and obstacle inhibiting their access to elementary education, women's participation in vocational, technical and professional education at different levels. Sarba Sikshya Abhijan, Midday Meal Schemes, Mahila Samukhya are being implemented for their improvement. Ministry of Social Justice and Empowerment is also implementing schemes of residential schools, Kanyasharmas for the SC and ST girls. The women's enrolment in universities and colleges is currently 39.94 per cent. There are five exclusive women's universities and 1,578 women colleges for them. The University Grants Commission (U.G.C.) has a number of schemes like setting of centres and cells for women studies, technological courses for women in women universities for undergraduate courses in engineering and technology, part-time research associateship for women, financial assistance to women's colleges for purchase of books, journals and equipments and also Day-care centres in universities etc.

There has been a remarkable stride in the rate of literacy since independence in India. The rate has increased from 18.33 per cent in 1951 to 65.38 in 2001 as per the census. The table below shows literacy rates among males and females, and the gap between the two since 1951.

Policies and Programmes

Literacy Rates in India

Census Year	*Total*	*Males*	*Females*	*Male-Female gap in Literacy Rate*
1951	18.33	27.16	8.86	18.30
1961	28.30	40.40	15.35	25.05
1971	34.45	45.96	21.97	23.98
1981	43.57	56.38	29.76	26.62
1991	52.21	64.13	39.29	24.84
2001	65.38	75.85	54.16	21.70

Source: Census of India-2001.

Within the framework of a democratic polity, our laws, development policies, plans and programmes have aimed at women's advancement in different spheres. The National Commission for Women established by an Act of Parliament in 1990 has to safeguard the rights and legal entitlements of women. The 73rd and 74th Amendments (1993) to the constitution of India have provided for seats in the local bodies. The 11th Plan strategy for gender balancing has taken care of the special needs of women such as clean cooking fuels, care for pregnant and nursing women etc.

Further, special measures will be taken to eliminate discrimination universalise education, eradicate illiteracy, create a gender sensitive educational system, increase enrolment and retention rates of girls and improve the quality of education to facilitate lifelong learning as well as development of occupation/ vocation and technical skills by women. Reservation of seats for girls in different educational institutions should be strictly followed. Reducing the gender gap in Secondary and Higher education would be a focus area. Special cares would be taken for their training in areas where they have special skills like arts and aesthetics, teaching, information and communication technology etc. The new approach identifies the instrumentality of empowering them organizing in groups, raising their level of awareness and providing them with social and economic support services.

Conclusion

In recent years, momentum has been gathering all over the world, demanding gender equality and push for equal representation of women in all spheres of activity. Education would surely liberate and equip women with ability to take control of her life, accomplish her dreams and enhance her status and stability. Educated women are Empowered women.

REFERENCES

Nanda, S.K.; *Pivotal Issues in Indian Education*, Kalyani Publisher, Ludhiana.

——; *National Policy on Education*, 1986/1992 MHRD, GOI, New Delhi.

Sharma, Sheetal; *Educated Women, Empowered Women*, Yojana, Oct. 2006 Vol. 50.

Vijayalakshmi. G.; *Women Empowerment Through Education*, Edutracks, Oct. 2003, Vol 3, No. 2.

28

WOMEN'S EDUCATION —At a Glance

—Arun Kumar Lenka

Women's Education is the call of the day. No family, no society and no nation can exist without women's education. The history of women's education is a picture of both light and shade with some outstanding achievements and outstanding failures. However, it is a fact that the child gets his first education from the mother. It has been said that the education of the child starts from the time of his conception in his mother's womb. The ancient Indian educationists believed in this ideal. Hence education of women is more important than that of men. In other words the significance of women's education can not be over emphasised.

It is true that we are in the process of modernising our educational system in view of the present day needs of our country. But let's have a peep into our women's education that has been incorporated in our existing system of education. In the vedic age, equality was given to the women. They enjoyed special opportunity and freedom. Both boys and girls received education in Ashrams and Gurukulas. In the age of Upanishadas, women were under no restriction to receive education. Dr. Radha Kumud Mukharjee observes that the educated virgin was considered to bring good fortune to the families of both her father and husband. The father's ambition was to see his daughter grow into a "Vidushi" or a learned woman. But in the later vedic period, the female education was on a constant and steady decline. The evolution of a false belief that women are inferior to men intellectually, gave a set-back to female education.

The Buddhist system of education was opposed to women's

education. The Buddha held that a woman had great responsibility at Home. So girls were not allowed admission in Buddhist monasteries. But later on, Lord Buddha agreed to their admission. Separate institutions were started for their education. Still it is a fact that women education was not encouraged during this period. Higher education was limited only to women belonging to the higher strata of society. In the 9th and the 10th century, due to a fall in the social and religious status of women, their education suffered further set-back.

During medieval India, due to the veil system among the muslim women, they could not attend maktabs or, rnadrasahs like male students. Only the rich people could educate their daughters by engaging private tuitors at home. There was no universal system of women education. Even there was no separate provision for the education of girls of general masses.

The East India Company hardly made any provision for state owned girl's school. Then it was purely a concern of the missionaries. But they could not wither the storm of opposition both social and religious. The solitary institution named after its founder, Bethune (Mr. J.E.D. Bethune), gave an impetus to the growth of similar private institutions all over India for progress of girls' education.

The next phase was marked after the Hunter Commission's Report, 1882. The Commission recommended that the women's education should receive a large share of public fund. A a result special attention was paid to the development of women's education both by the government and private bodies.

Some active steps were taken by government during 1902 - 1917 for the improvement of women education. New plans were devised, separate schools were started, inspectresses were appointed, prizes were offered to girls and steps were taken to attract ladies to the teaching profession. The above measures gave great encouragement to women's education and in 1904, Mrs. Annie Besant established the Central Hindu Girls' School at Banaras with the object of imparting western education to girls, quite separately from boys.

Due to the political and social awakening in the country, the social status of women had begun to show an upward trend and their role in socio-political field had began to be recognised. In social reform and political awakening many women took active part and did pioneering work. All these factors gave impetus to women's education and as a result the enrolment in different educational institutions increased considerably.

Since independence, there is no doubt that women education in India is in progress but still it is lagging far behind when compared to other countries. Still millions of women are deprived of this basic right. Pandit Jawaharlal Nehru remarked, "Education of a boy is the education of one person, but education of a girl is the education of the entire family".

After independence several commissions and committees were appointed to suggest measures for the improvement of education in general. University Education Commission appointed in 1948-49 recommended for the improvement of women's education at higher education level. Dr. Radhakrishnan very emphatically stated, "Women are human being and have as much right to full development as men have. The position of women in any society is true index of its cultural and spiritual level."

The secondary education commission (1952 - 53) states that "To promote the pattern of society that we envisage for the future, the expansion of girl education must take place with boy's education".

Regarding the education of girls, Kothari Commission (1964 - 66) states that in the modem world, the role of the woman goes much beyond the home and the bringing up of children. She is now adopting a career of her own and sharing equally with the man, the responsibility for the development of society in all its aspects.

A National Committee on Women's Education has provided the following recommendations :

a. Priority should be given to women's education in the further programme of the development of education in the country.

b. Discrimination between the education as boys and girls should be curbed and both should expand on an equal footing.

c. The national government should encourage states to launch various programmes associated with the development of women's education.

d. Proper facilities and protection should be provided to women teachers serving in rural areas.

Besides the above recommendations of the various commissions and committees, several other schemes have been launched by the Central Government and State Government to meet the need of the educationally disavantaged namely Operation Black Board (OB), District Primary Education Programme (DPEP), Education Guarantee Scheme (EGS),. Integrated Child Development Scheme (ICDS), Sarva Sikshya Abhijan (SSA), Mahila Vikas Sambaya Nigam (MVSN), Balika Samrudhi Yojana, etc. These and many such schemes adopted by the Government, empower women socially, economically and educationally.

29

WOMEN EDUCATION AND EMPOWERMENT

—Avarani Nanda

The education of girls and women is an integral part of national development. Education, in the presnt day context, is perhaps the single most important means for individuals to improve personal endowment, build capacity levels, and overcome constraints. It enlarges their available set of opportunities and choices for a sustained development. Women, who comprise half of the country's population, need to be viewed as productive members of the society showing equal authority and responsibility of being citizens. Educational attainment is, without doubt, the most fundamental pre-requisite for empowering women in all spheres of society. 'Empower' refers to multi-dimensional capacity and competency building among women to be equal partners of life. Increasing a woman's educational level and control over financial resources can improve her status.

The pace of education is a tool for empowering women. Various authors and researchers have focused on different aspects of women empowerment. The entire effort of empowering women is to help them to exercise their rights in decision-making in every sphere, i.e. social, economic, political aspects of life at the family or societal level including a right over their own biological functions and needs. The parameters of education for women's empowerment range from enhancing self-esteem and confidence of women, building a positive image of women by recognizing their contribution to the society, polity and economy.

The programme of action of ICPD, in Cairo, 1994, stated,- "Advancing gender equality, equity and empowerment of women and the elimination of all kinds of violence against women and ensuring women's ability to control their own fertility are corner stones and development related programmes. The declaration on POA (Programme of action) of the world summit for social development, held in Copenhagen in March 1995, called for equal educational and work opportunities for women. The fourth world conference on women held in Beijing in 1995 emphasizes education of girls and young women as the key intervention for the improvement of women. The National Population Policy (NPP), 2000 enunciated by the government of India has given due recognition to women empowerment and gender issues as a path to population stabilization.

Better education expands economic opportunities for women and helps in decision-making about themselves, their families and communities. Therefore, government of India launched the National Literacy Mission (NLM) in 1988 as an important part of National Policy of education. Empowerment eliminates variable subjugation, drudgery at domestic work of women and develops consciousness about their own position in the society. It encourages to take steps against all kinds of male violence in a patriarchal society and directs for greater utilization of capacities in economic productive activities.

Literacy campaign has heightened social awareness among women, motivated and encouraged women learners to educate their children and girls by enrolling them in formal schools. Literacy has thus actively promoted gender equity and has sought to empower them. More access to information and knowledge empower the women to take decisions on their reproductive rights. Therefore, it is associated with higher contraceptive use, lower fertility and effort on population growth. Moreover, infant mortality rate is lower in families in which women are better educated, prevents more births and protects mother's health and quality of life.

There is also good reason to relate remarkable high life expectancy levels in Kerala to its educational achievement particularly of women and on the other side to relate the low life expectancy of some of the northern Indian states due to backwardness in female education.

In conclusion, education is a vital input for empowerment of women. Therefore, empowerment of women has to be comprehensive enough to ensure political, social and financial aspects. Social patterns, institutions, community and influential leaders should act as social agents to support programmes of literacy, education and health care of girl child and women and provide necessary back up for the employment of women. They should be provided access to information and choice in the different fields. Women being empowered and taking control of their fertility are able to invest relatively more in a smaller number of beloved children, trying to prepare them for a better future. So it is rightly said "Educating a man is educating an individual, educating a woman is educating a family".

PROBLEMS OF WOMEN EDUCATION AND SOLUTION

—YUDHISTIR KHATUA

All Nations of the world have attained greatness, by paying proper respect to the women. The countries which did not respect the women have never become great. Indian women are as capable as any women in any part of the world. Though constitution has granted special privileges to women practically they are kept much behind men in various activities. Hence women should be given equal rights with men in every field according to their interests and demands. However, during last fifty five years India has produced many great women in the field of science, literature, politics and social service.

Significance of Women Education

Educated mothers at home can successfully impart true education to their children. As human beings women have as much right as men have for development. They can adopt career of their own and share equally with men. The education of girls should be given emphasis not only on grounds of social justice but also from the point of view of social transformations.

Problems of Women Education

Many committees and commissions have expressed concern regarding slow progress of women education in our country. They are as follows :

1. The University Education Committee (1948-49).
2. Smt. Durgabai Deshmukh Committee (1959).
3. Smt. Hansa Meheta Committee (1962).
4. M. Bhaktavatsalam Committee.

5. Education Commission (1964-66).
6. Resolution on the National Policy on Education (1968).
7. Report of the Committee on the status of women in India (1974).
8. Challenge of Education (1985).
9. National Policy on Education (1986).
10. Programme of Action (1986).

The commitees have found out the problems of women education from time to time. The problems are :

1. Economic Problems of Rural People.
2. Lack of Positive attitude of rural people towards girls' education.
3. Lack of proper educational facilities in village areas.
4. Insufficienf women teachers.
5. Lack of proper inspection and guidance.
6. Lack of adequate incentives to parents and children.
7. Lack of suitable curriculum.
8. Lack of adequate separate institutions for girls.

The Government Effort for Women Education

The State Government have done a lot for expansion of women education. The administration of women education is Just like that of education for boys. The inspectors and other Government officers supervise Girls education. In 1959 a National council for women education was established for looking after Girls education. It has recommended that Girls education should be treated as separate Unit of education and state government should establish Advisory council for women education and there should be a Joint Director for women education.

Higher Education

Some necessary changes are also being introduced in the curriculum in order to suit their interests and aptitudes. Some girls are attracted towards professional courses like medical, engineering, teaching and nursing etc.

Secondary Education

The growth of women education at secondary stage has become satisfactory. The curriculum has also been suitably modified as to suit their special requirements and tastes.

Primary Education

Primary education is the foundation for the development of Secondary and Higher education. It has been estimated that only 30 percent of the Girls of primary school reach the fifth class. Both central and state Governments are taking keen interest for enforcing this education for Girls up to the secondary stage.

Suggestive Measures

The following suggestive measures may be undertaken for the development of women education :

1. Free uniforms and free books to the needy and deserving children should be provided.
2. Attendance scholarships which serve as a compensation to the parents should be given. It would help for reduction of wastage and stagnation.
3. Mid-day-meals should be available free of charges.
4. To study the problems relating to women's education a thorough research should be taken up.
5. Separate schools for girls at middle and high school stage should be established where needed.
6. School mothers in co-education primary schools should be appointed.
7. Nursery classes wherever possible should be opened.
8. Public opinion in favour of girls education should be created.
9. Close co-operation with activities of women social workers, state council of girls education and district organisations. Radio, press, Films, Posters, Parent-Teacher Associations, Adequate literature for popular reading of rural people should be available.
10. At least one primary school within walking distance of a child should be established.
11. Hostel for girls at the middle and high school stage should be setup.
12. Maintenance stipends to girls hostelers should be given.
13. Subsidised transport facilities wherever necessary and possible be provided.
14. A large number of training institutions should be provided for women.

15. Condensed courses should be started.
16. A large number of quarters for women teachers should be provided.
17. All women teachers serving in rural areas should be given rural allowance.
18. Special stipends should be provided to girls in high and higher secondary schools with aptitude for teaching.
19. Wherever possible husbands and wives should be posted in the same place even if they work in different departments of the Government.
20. Free training should be imparted with stipends.
21. In service education should be provided.
22. There should be increase in the number of inspecting officers particularly in backward areas.
23. Provision of adequate transport for all district women inspecting officers.
24. Adequate office staff and equipment, residential facilities to all women officers at all levels, adequate funds to state councils should be provided.
25. Opening adult literacy classes in large numbers, teaching of simple skills like sewing, knitting, handicrafts and knowledge of basic principles of health and food habits should be imparted.
26. Development of positive attitudes towards community living, family planning, superstitions, castes etc. should be made.
27. The number of attendance scholarships should be more.
28. The allowance of school mothers should be enhanced so that qualified women may be attracted to take up the work.
29. The maintenance stipends should be increased keeping price rise in the mind.
30. The sanitary facilities should be adequately provided in co-educational primary schools.
31. Larger allocation of funds should be made in budget for construction of hostels for girls.
32. Steps should be taken to improve the instruction of home economics, teaching of music and fine arts and financial assistance to these courses.
33. The universities should review periodically the provision they

have made for the courses.

34. Co-education should be adopted as the general pattern at the elementary stage.
35. At the secondary and college stage there should be full freedom to the managements and parents either to evolve common institutions or to establish separate ones for girls.
36. Steps should be taken to appoint women teachers in secondary and university institutions where girls are actually attending.

The women have been playing key roles in social and economic life of the countries. Hence greater attention will have to be paid to the problems of training and development of women. Their education needs priority not only from the points of view of social justice but also because it accelerates social transformation.

REFERENCES

Aggarwal J.C., *Development and Planning of Modern Education.*

Choube S.P., *Problems of Indian Education.*

Dhanpat Rai & Sons, *Development Planning and Problems of Indian Education.*

Mukherjee S.N., *Education in India : To-day and Tomorrow.*

Sharma Ram Nath and Rajendra K. Sharma, *Problems of Education in India.*

31

THE ROLE OF WOMEN EDUCATORS IN STRENGTHENING MORAL AND SPIRITUAL VALUES IN THE AGE OF GLOBALISM

—JYOSTNA SAHOO

Globalism today is being accepted as synonym for progress, scientific break through and technological revolution. With its long strides, it is being taken as a model description of the new utilitarian thrust in our approach to education. The traditional approach to education has been to see its utility and purpose in terms of social and moral awareness, to impart beauty and dignity to life and also to provide with a code of conduct for a good social and moral order.

The development of Science and Technology has brought the world together. But it has not brought union in thoughts for the betterment of human race. They are still poles apart as before. The contained culture growing in big cities has been driving individuals away from each other. Self respect, affection, love, togetherness, regard and respect for elderly persons and values like these are fast fading away from the society. Knowledge, Learning and sophistication are making individuals self-centered instead of widening the range of their thinking abilities. Presence of old parents in the family is becoming inconveniences instead of a building force. Once upon a time they were looked up for guidance and now they themselves have been in difficulty.

It is there that the Education system and the women educators as a whole have a very important role to play. The invasion of the western thoughts. too has made matters more complicated. The present generation, barring exception here and there, derive pleasure in adopting western life style, than sticking to our own. Is our culture so slippery? Are our eternal values, taught by our age-old religion, ineffective as to be easily conquered by other religions, which are of recent origin?

Therefore, we need to reshape our curriculum. We must introduce lessons on our own tradition, culture and heritage. Respect, love, affection for the parents and family, regard for the elders are now required to be taught. Our curriculum needs amendment to include lessons on the importance of cleanliness, humility, honesty, tolerance, patience, fearlessness, clarity in thought and action, truthfulness, cheerfulness, sense of appreciation, in day-to-day life.

From the early years of life the human being is brought up by a woman, who is his/her mother. A mother sustains and maintains family life, loves, serves and sacrifices everything for her baby. So it is nicely stated that mother is the first teacher of a human being. She acts in multifarious roles as daughter, sister, niece in her father's house and a wife, a mother and in-laws in her husbands house. The destiny of a nation is moulded and fashioned through its education and in this the education of women has a strategic importance Nepolion said "give me good mothers, I will give you a good nation." Many great men have expressed in their biographies that they had become so due to the influence of their mothers.

The 2001 census shows that in India 65.38% persons, 75.85% males and 54.16% females are literate. According to Human Development Report 2001. India ranks 105 in Gender Related Development (GD1) and 95 in Gender Empower Measure (GEM). Government of India has declared 2001 is the year for women empowerment. In this connection one question comes to mind; Are the women powerless or incapable, so the question of empowerment arises?

Actually, in true sense empowerment is a process of enhancing power or capacities. It is a process of energizing, activating, encouraging enlightening one with extra power on vigour to action and knowledge, skills and abilities.

If we analyse these things in detail we can come to the conclusion that women are most efficient and can bring changes in our society by their sincere efforts. Both Education and the Women educators can contribute a lot in building the nation.

- The women educators from the pre-primary stage to

University level can influence and reshape the conduct of the children on one hand and manifest erosion in observance of eternal, social, moral and ethical values on the other.

- They should practise and promote moral and spiritual values in personal and professional life so as to lay new foundation for a just and fair society.
- They should work with determination to remove conflicts, crime, social evils, violence, from the society.
- They should educate the children about the importance of divine virtues like peace, love, tolerance, co-operation, unity, etc., which are required to build a better world.

Humanism should be the motto of education in all circumstances. The society should recognize the innate virtues and qualities of women, so as to make them torch bearers to enlighten and blaze the path leading to the destination of liberation and fruition.

Although a large number of educational institutions, both Government and Private have been opened. it is ironical that there is growing deterioration of values also. The role of teacher is great to fulfill the lacuna; otherwise there will be the crisis of character.

The importance of choosing women educators is to instill awareness about moral and spiritual values by quoting profusely from the scriptures, customs, festivals, places of worship, folk lore and folk tales in India right from the ancient time till this day.

Lastly the provision of six-point action plan may be implemented in our educational institutions.

- Need for restoration of ancient glory to the teacher for building up of better 21st century.
- Provision of spiritual knowledge and meditation in educational institutions.
- Bringing relevant changes and amendment in the curricula of students, teachers at all levels and formulation of different syllabi for total development of child.
- Bringing awareness about value-based education among the different professions and professionals in the society.
- Giving complete co-operation to achieve the goal and crisis of Human Rights declaration (1995-2004).
- Bringing awareness to the citizens about meaning and concepts of national integration and harmony.

It is the woman who in turn, lends her full support to the man in every walk of life. She plays the role of a mother and takes care of man as a child, teaches him good habits, gives shape to his raw imagination, and also hones his intellectual skills to make him a successful, responsible and well-behaved individual so as to contribute significantly to the progress of the society.

REFERENCES

Gupta, N.L., (2000) : *Women Education Through the Ages,* Concept Publishing Company, New Delhi.

Puram, R.K., (2004) : *Independence Day Special,* Yojana ,Vol - 48, Page 21, New Delhi.

Reddy, G.S., (2002) : *Women Empowerment Teacher Education,* Edutracks, Vol. No. 7, April pp. 13-14.

Venkataish. S., (2001l) : *Women Education,* Anmol Publication Pvt. Ltd., New Delhi.

32

EMERGENCE OF THE WOMEN EDUCATION

—Debi Prasanna Barik

In India we have different views regarding women and their position in society . In early times on the one hand women were respected while on the other hand they were considered as non-independent and weak human being, protected by their father when young, by husband in her youth and by son in her old age. The traditional India had also seen a woman only as a member of the family or group-as daughters, wives and mothers and not as an individual with an identity or right of her own. Majority of them were custodians of the family and responsible for the well-being of children inculcating in them the cultural values and very few of them participate in social functions outside the family. Gradually with the growth of modernization, Urbanization, Industrialization and rising prices women began to came out of the 'Lakshman Rekha' of their house and work outside for wage or salary.

An analysis of the various facts relating to the status of women in India reveals that though we are progressing towards the 21st century, a lot of needs to be done for the upliftment of women, who constitute 498.7 million according to 2001 census, represent 48.2 per cent of country's population i.e. 1,027 million.

The special provisions for women in Indian constitution were result of social reform movement which began in 19th century emphasizing improvement of women's status. Social reformers like Raja Rammohan Ray, Mahatma Gandhi etc. agreed that no substantial change could be achieved as long as women were deprived of opportunities of self-development and participation. By recognising the unequal social position of women, the constitution of India guarantees several rights for women in it's Articles — 14, 15(I), 15(3)1, 16, 39(9), 39(d), 243D(3), 243D(4) & 243 T(3).

The status of woman in India can be improved only by empowering women socio-economically. Women empowerment is a multi-dimensional process, which enables the women individually and collectively to realise their full identity and powers in all spheres of life. It consists of greater access to knowledge and resources, greater autonomy in decision making, enable them to have greater ability to plan their lives by avoiding customs, believes and practices of the society. Researches in the field of women education show that in families where the women are educated, social evils such as illiteracy of girl children, child labour, early marriage and other superstitions are much less. When a woman is educated, it is in effect the whole family is educated. In order to ensure better participation of women in the developmental process of the nation, the entire population is to be involved to create a sense of awareness about values and the need to empower women through quality education.

In this context Pandit Jawaharlal Nehru says -

> "In order to awaken the people it is the women who has to be awakened, once she is on move, the family moves, the village moves, the nation moves."

The status of the women in many parts of our country is very low as they denied all privileges including education. This has led to the failure of the efforts put in by the Government to achieve total adult literacy. The overall literacy rate increased from 18.3% in 1951 to 65.38%in 2001, where female literacy rate accounted for 54.16 %. The highest literacy rate is in Kerala i.e., 90.92% and lowest is in Bihar i.e., 47.53% Kerala contributes 3.10% of the total population while Bihar contributes 8.07%. The Government launched the National Literacy Mission (NLM) with the objective of achieving total adult literacy in 1988 among 80 million adults in the age group of 15-35 years by 1995. The target was furthered in 1998-99 to benefit 100 million adults by 2005. 561 districts in the country have been covered and 91.53 million people have become literate in the last decade. The total literacy campaign has covered 166 districts, the post literacy campaign in 290 districts and 152 distircts have been covered by continuing Education Programme in our country. Evening schools are imparting education to those people who find it difficult to attend formal schools because of their occupations. For furthering their education, they could seek admission in to the open school or National Open School. The Indira Gandhi National Open University (IGNOU) was set up in 1985 with the intention of providing degree programmes along with vocational education under the distance education scheme.

There has been a rapid progress in girls education since independence. The enrolment of girls in classes I to V increased 8 times i.e., from 53.8 lakhs in 1951 to 449 lakhs in 1993 and in classes VI to VIII was 28 times. i.e., from 5.4 lakhs in 1951 to 150 lakhs in 1993. The enrolment ratio of girls to total enrolment during 1992-93 was 43 per cent at Primary stage, 39 per cent at the middle stage and 34 per cent at the higher secondary stage. Steps have been taken by the Government through some new programmes like DPEP, SSA, EGS etc. to achieve the goal of Universalization of Elementary Education.

The gross women enrolment in higher education was less than 10% at the time of independence and it has increased to 39.84% i.e., 35,14,450 out of total, enrolment 8821095 in 2001-2002. Approximately 90% women are enrolled in general education and only 10% of them are in Technical disciplines. More and more number of women ITI and Polytechnics with new trades and disciplines suits the present day needs have been set up by the Government and private bodies.

The women of today have two priorities - home and work place. As both are of equal demand, the indispensable support of their husband and children enable them to maintain balance in both the worlds. It is found that women are more determined and committed towards family, education and profession. Hence, parents should not create a gender bias between their children. Educated girls are also known to support their parents in their old age when their brothers fail to do so. Dowry system can also be put to an end if educated women stand up against the system. Thus, education of the women would mean the emancipation of women and the social development of the nation.

33

WOMEN PARTICIPATION IN HIGHER EDUCATION

—Akadasi Senapati

An Indian woman, endowed with traditional culture and values, becomes a polished diamond on getting modern education and professional skill. An educated, employed woman with her natural traditional goodness and grace is the ideal woman. Mahatma Gandhi believed in the fact that educating the single woman is equal to educating the entire family . Modern system of education is expected to bring in all round personality development in women, providing them a new vision worldview. helping her to adjust to the needs of her family and the community.

It is only education, which provides her power to fight against any form of evil Despite of many debates, discussions, conferences and conventions, women are still more likely to be poor, malnourished and illiterate than men. In spite of having a massive system of higher education, they have less access to employment and independence in social, economic and political spectrum.

Higher education can only provide women with more prestigious forms of jobs and professional employment which clearly depends on the access of higher education for women. Education should be a particular ground to train the women to become independent, self-reliant and self-conscious. The position of women in higher education has become' a matter of interest, if not of concern, all over the world. The present paper is targeted to highlight the women's position in higher education of India and some need of rethinking to raise their participation in higher education.

A survey carried out by commonwealth Higher Education Management Service shows that in the commonwealth as a whole, women's representation is only about 25 %. We have to look at the problem of under representation of women in higher education as a global problem and not something unique to India.

In the past fifty years, several milestones have been crossed to high up the education of women. Special Commissions and Committees were set up to assess the progress of women education and propose suitable interventions to promote their participation. Since independence, the promotion of women's enrolment to total enrolment, has been rapidly increasing from 10 % in 1950- 51 to 39.84% in 2001-02.

Table 33.1 : Enrolment of Women in Higher Education

Sl.No.	*Year*	*Total Women Enrolment*	*Percentage of Women*
1.	1950-51	43,126	10.9
2.	1960-61	1,70,455	16.2
3.	1970-71	6,55,822	21.9

Source: University News (44) (33), 2006, (Aug. 14-20).

Table 33.2 : Enrolment of Women in Total Enrolment in Higher Education

Sl.No.	*Year*	*Total Enrolment*	*Total Women Enrolment*	*Percentage of Women*
1.	1995-1996	65,74,005	23,63,607	36
2.	1996-1997	68,42,598	25,14,511	37
3.	1997-1998	72,60,418	27,22,062	37
4.	1998-1999	77,05,520	29,32,993	38
5.	1999-2000	80,50,607	31,12,090	39
6.	2000-2001	83,99,443	33,06,410	39.4
7.	2001-2002	88,21,095	35,14,450	39.84

Source: UGC Annual Report, 2001-2002.

The above tables reflect the steady increase of women in higher education. Only 6 % of women reach the level of college education and beyond due to heavy dropout at the school stage. The rough calculations suggested that the rate of increase in enrolment of women in higher education is just 06% per year and the state as a whole witnessed only 3.84 % growth in women's participation in higher education within the last seven years. Because of the socio-cultural mindset girls are not given education, particularly higher education.

In India, higher education programme is classified in terms of faculty. So far as the choice of subject is concerned, the maximum number of women choose general subject like Arts. The faculty-wise distribution of women enrolment during (2001-02) is given in Table 33.3.

Table 33.3 given below indicates that approximately 90 % of women were enrolled in general education consisting of Arts, Science and Commerce. But only 10 % were enrolled in professional and technical disciplines which focus upon practical and occupational skills and opportunities.

Table 33.3 : Faculty-wise Women Participation in Higher Education (2001-2002)

Sl.No.	*Faculty*	*Enrolment*	*Percentage*
1.	Arts	18,20,134	51.79
2.	Science	6,99,376	19.90
3.	Commerce/Management	5,81,993	16,56
4.	Education	59,394	1.69
5.	Engineering/Technology	1,31,792	3.75
6.	Medicine	1,23,006	3.50
7.	Agriculture	9,137	0.26
8.	Veterinary Science	3,163	0.09
9.	Law	56,934	1.62
10.	Others	29,521	0.84
	Total	35,14,450	100

Source: UGC Annual Report, 2001-2002.

There has been a substantial increase in number of women colleges during the last decades. In 1991 number of women Colleges was 994 only, while it increased to 1600 in 2001. Besides these the women universities have been established and they are playing an important role in becoming effective instruments of empowerment of women.

Problems of Women Participation in Higher Education

- Entry of women to higher education were over represented by urban areas and hailing from affluent background.

Researches proved that, higher the education and employment level of the parents, higher is the participation of women in higher education. However, the education of women is determined by the parental economic condition.

- Marriage poses another critical problem for women's participation in higher education, specifically among rural Indian women. Higher the level of education of the girls, lower is the chance to get a suitable mate. It is thought so, because the groom invariabley to be better educated than the bride and higher the level of education of the bridegroom, higher is the expectation in terms of dowry. In spite of the laws against dowry practice the stark reality is transparent and this often makes parents unwilling to send their girls for higher education although they might have shown necessary aptitude and competence.
- Often it is witnessed that women students in colleges and Universities opt for light subjects such as music, home science and liberal arts rather than physics or environmental studies indicating a kind of sexual stereotyping in higher education in India Their low participation in science and engineering due to the traditional practices between the sexes encourage boys to opt for science and technical subjects and girls to opt for liberal subjects like arts.

  It is true that there is an increasing trend towards women opting for administrative, management and computer examinations demonstrating a marked improvement in the choice of hard subjects, but the number is still small.
- The sex-role ideology directed by the traditional norm of patriarchy is another hindrance to the higher rate of women participation in higher education. Most of us think if a girl wants higher education to enhance her opportunities for a full-time career then family and children must be neglected for her. It is the general view of the common man that women education has no return value with respect to economic aspect of their family.

Suggestions

- At graduation level new courses should be designed which are job-oriented, need oriented and relevant to the needs of the society.
- Women should be provided equal opportunities in holding

high positions in Universities, industries, civil services or other important organization in nation building.

- University should start giving adequate scholarships to the outstanding women students in different disciplines. However, UGC has declared that the scholarships would be awarded to the rank holder women students in different disciplines.
- By reserving seats for women students in different disciplines, the parents will certainly motivate to send their girls for higher education.
- Courses like interior decoration, fashion designing/ technology, beauticians, guidance and counselling, script writing for media programmes, computer hardware and software, technical know-how of electronic gadgets etc. can enable the women participation for jobs in offices and self-employment.
- Women from the lower social classes still graduate only in general courses, nursing, social work etc. Some deliberate measures are to be taken to encourage professional education among girls of lower socio-economic class so that women do not continue to cluster around a few occupations like teaching etc.
- It is suggested that adequate reservation may be provided to women in admission to professional and other courses in higher education. However, such a reservation can be a motivating factor only when it is linked to future benefits like women employment and economic independence. This can facilitate women to think of alternative life styles and their perception towards the life.
- Incentives should be given to women and women institutions by way of free education and liberal grants.

Conclusion

Education is the key to make women self-reliant and self-confident. Education in general and higher education in particular is expected to uphold the dignity of women as equal partners in societal development. In this direction it is not enough that mere planning, policies and legislation will serve, but it is simultaneously necessary to mobilize a favorable and co-operative public opinion. The participation of women in higher education will certainly transform their attitude and values. To conclude with the recommendations of

NPE (1986)—as education is one of the basic rights of a human being, irrespective of sex, religion and community, it is necessary to provide adequate opportunities to women to get suitable higher education and improve their status.

Last but not least, higher education should help women to bring out the best talents available in them in to the main stream of the development process. The higher:education system should have an inbuilt mechanism for empowerment.

REFERENCES

Devendra, K., (1994); *Changing Status of Women in India*, Vikash Publishing House Pvt. Ltd., New Delhi.

Chatterji, Shoma A., (1993); Ajanta Publications, Delhi.

Desai, N. & Patel, V., (1990) ; Popular Prakashan Pvt. Ltd., Bombay.

—; *University News, Vol. 43, No.-6, Feb. 07-13, 2005*, AIU, New Delhi.

—; *University News, (44) (33), Aug. 14-20, 2006*, AIU, New Delhi.

—; *University News, Vol. 44*, No.-24, June-12-18, *2006* AIU, New Delhi.

WOMEN EMPOWERMENT —Role of Education

—LEENA ROY

Introduction

Our women have so far been confined to the hearth, but a time has come for their upliftment and emancipation. Our Government and parliament have passed several Acts and Bills for developing their status and dignity. A number of committees, commissions, conferences, seminars, discussions are also throwing light on different aspects of women education. But still women do not have equitable access to literacy, education, food, nutrition, health, employment or in the political and economic decision making process. Here the need is to empower women. In this context, women empowerment is a burning issue and the role of education in this regard is vital.

Our women have a very great part to play in the progress of our country. In the apron strings of women is hidden the revolutionary energy which can establish paradise on this earth (Rajendra Prasad).

So it is time that all of us have to give a serious thought to empower women. This paper unfolds a few major aspects that need to be pondered over and addressed in this emerging social order.

Theorising Women Empowerment

It is a process of assisting the women to recognise their inner power, the quality, competency, excellence, talents and make them developed to make right choice. Women empowerment is to endow them with the power to execute their will, the will to with stand in social economic, political and educational field and to assert their right to arrest the challenge of life. Women empowerment means they should be authorized to take their own decision and develop in them self-confidence, self-respect, positive attitude, own decision making, equity and feeling of equality. The various dimensions of women empowerment are self confidence, self esteem, self image, self reliance, self sufficiency and self dependence.

The other dimensions of women empowerment are :

- Making them aware of their right, duties and Privileges.
- Developing critical thinking and feeling of equality.
- Involving women in different spheres.
- Providing freedom for taking own decisions.
- Participating in the process of bringing about social changes.

There are various obstacles ensuring women empowerment. They are social, economical, physical, administrative and educational respectively.

The Social obstacles are -

- Tradition ridden Social customs, Gender stereotyping and Conservatism of parents.

The Economical obstacles are -

- Poverty, higher of the burden of dowry and engagement of girls in otherwise way.

The Physical obstacles are -

- Poor transport facility, lack of physical facilities and regional disparities.

The administrative obstacles are -

- Lack of dissemination of proper knowledge, lack of enthusiasm and interest of the officials in charge of education and lack of appreciation of the need for women education.

The Educational obstacles are -

- Illiteracy, limited employment opportunities and non-attractive formal learning institution.

Women Empowerment : Role of Education

Education will be used as an agent of basic change in the status of women. In order to neutralize the accumulated distortions of the past; there will be a well-conceived edge in favour of women. The National Educational System will play a positive, interventionist role in the empowerment of women. It will foster the development of new values through redesigning curricula, textbooks, the training and orientation of teachers, decision makers administrators and the active involvement of educational institution. This will be an act of faith and social engineering. Women's studies will be promoted as a part of various courses and educational institutions encouraged to take up active programmes to further women's development. (N.P.E. 1986 on Edu of women)

Strategies of Education for Women Empowerment

Following are some of the strategies which should be undertaken for women empowerment.

- Community awareness programme, parent education programme.
- Active and positive involvement of educational institutions.
- Training and orientation of teachers, other education, personnel, decision makers administrators.
- Requirement of more lady teachers.
- Common core-curriculum.
- Re-orientation of text book.
- Availability of funds.
- Universalisation of education.
- Special schemes, plans made by autonomous bodies of Government like U.G.C., N.C.E.R.T., S.C.E.R.T., A.I.C.T.E., N.I.E.P.A.
- Support service to rural girls.
- Village education committee, Mahila Samiti.
- Adult educaton, Nonformal education.
- National Literacy Mission.
- Technical and vocational education.
- Higher Education.
- Role of N.G.O.

Conclusion

Empowering women is an extremely complex and challenging task. It can be achieved not by careful planning or managing our efforts tactfully, but only when all the citizens realize their responsibility in this respect collectively.

DEVELOPMENT OF WOMEN EDUCATION—Emerging Issues

—NAMITA DASH

In the rapidly changing era of globalization, development of women education in higher learning is undergoing profound change in their scope, function and organisations. Since independence, much stress has been given on education for women at all levels including higher education, keeping par with advanced countries of the world.

Before independence in the field of higher education, the enrolment of Brahmin girls was higher than other Non-Brahmin communities. It stood at 34.07% by 1946-47. The growth in enrolment of Non-Brahmin community stood at 20.5% due to the development of co-educational facilities. Among the Christian communities the growth in girls education was negligible due to some socio-economic factors. They were accounted as 0.5%. As far as Muslim community is concerned their percentage was nil in 1921-22. It increased up to 2.4% by 1946-47.

After independence University Education Commission (1948-49), Secondary Education Commission (1952-53), Kothari Commission (1964-66), N.P.E. (1986) and Plan and Programme (1992) emphasised on women education.

After independence total enrolment of women in higher education in India increased gradually which has been reflected in Table 35.1.

Over a Period of time, noticeable emphasis on women's education can also be seen.

The number of women's college has recorded a substantial increase. In 2001-02 India had 1500 women's colleges with

Table 35.1 : Enrolment of Women in Higher Education in India

Year	*No. of Women enrolled*	*Percentage*
1950	43,126	10.9
1960	1,70,455	16.2
1970	6,55,822	21.9
1996	21,91,138	34.1
1997	25,14,551	36.7
2001-02	--	37.65
2002-03	--	40.05

enrolment of women standing at 37.65 per cent of the total students' enrolment. However girls in general have shown more inclination towards non-professional stream as is evident from the fact that 87 per cent of the enrolment in this category is in Arts, Science, and Commerce. While only 13 per cent of the total girl students have made their way to the professional courses. The highest enrolment of the women has been reported at 56.70 per cent for Goa closely followed by Kerala (55.9%) while Bihar reported the lowest at 24.45% in 2001-2002. In India there are five Women Universities like

1. SNDT Women's University, Mumbai.
2. Mother Teresa Women's University, Kodaikanal.
3. Sri Padmavathy Mahila Vishwa Vidyalaya, Tirupati.
4. Banasthall Vidyapith, Jaipur.
5. Avinashilingam Institute for Home Science and Higher Education for Women Deemed University, Coimbatore.

Now in 2002-03 there are 1650 women colleges in India.

Emerging Issues on Women Education

Inspite of the constitutional guarantees and positive intention of the government to promote highe, education of women, some emerging issues are creating a problem for its development which are listed below :

- Poor economic conditions of the family.
- Conservative illiteracy, ignorance of the parents.
- Early marriage and the purdah system.
- Inadequate transport facilities in rural areas.
- Lack of qualified teachers.

- Lack of residential facilities.
- Unsuitable curriculum.
- Wastage and stagnation.
- Population explosion.
- Shortage of Colleges & Universities.
- Fear of girls molestation, urbanisation and modernisation.
- Declining public expenditure on women higher education.
- Higher rate of donation for Engineering and Medical science.
- Employement crisis.
- Lack of scope in developing I.T. skill.
- Inadequate research facilities.

Conclusion

Considering the various emerging issues in the way of development of women education efforts should be made from the side of Government as well as the general public to over come them in the light of the recommendations made by the Commissions and Committees appointed from time to time. Without the development of half of the society the development of the society can not be imagined.

WOMEN EDUCATION—Issues and Strategies

—DHARANIDHAR SAHOO

Introduction

The destiny of a nation is moulded and fashioned through its education and the education of women has strategic importance. The contribution of Indian women has been crediable to the country's development process since independence. It has been a source for reaching national goals. In recent years it is observed that women are lagging behind a great deal both in availing developmental opportunities and in participating developmental process due to various impediments. Women, constituting about fifty percent of India's population receive only a small portion of development process. So the importance of women education was urgently felt by the educationists, planners, policy makers and administrators in the present day.

Importance of Women Education After Independence

After Independence Several Commissions and Committees were appointed to suggest measures for the improvement of education of women.

A. University Education Commission (1948-49) gave stress on the various aspects of women education.

B. The Five Year Plans have been paying special attention to women's welfare.

C. National Committee on Women Education was set up in 1958 to consider the whole question of women education.

D. Durgabai Desmukh Committee (1959) appointed by the national government with regard to the education of girls.

E. Hansa Mehta Committee (1962) gave a priority on the curriculum of girl's education.

F. Bhaktavatsalam Committee (1963) was appointed to investigate the causes for lack of public support for girl's education particularly in rural areas.

G. National Council for Women's Education (1964) was appointed to look into the problems of women's education.

H. Kothari Commission (1964-66) gave stress on the expansion and improvement of women education.

I. The National Policy on Education (1986) was concerned about the status and education of women in the country.

J. National Policy on Education Reveiw Committee (1990) considered women education to be a vital component of the overall strategy of securing equity and social justice in education.

K. Programme of Action (1992) had also made a valuable suggestion regarding the development of women's education.

Emerging Issues/Obstacles on the Way of Women Education

The education of women is an integral part of national development. But in present time majority of women still suffer from drastic in equalities. There is still a dearth of systematic planning which pose a great challenge before the country. There are a number of issues on the way of women's education. They are Population explosion, illiteracy, regional disparties in women's literacy, large dropout rates among girl students, less parental education, low economic background, inadequate communication facilities, in equality in the education level of both male and female, blind religious belief, inadequate educational institutions in rural areas.

Effective Measures for the Development of Women Education

The following are some of the measures for the development of education among women or girls.

- Both government and non-government organisations should act jointly and proceed in a planned manner with regard to the education of women/girls.
- Co-education should be made popular at primary stage.
- Social education centres should be established in rural areas for women.
- Functional curriculum should be evolved for adult women.

- Vocational training for women should be planned.
- An awareness of the need for women's education should be spread.
- Women study centres should be organised in different levels of education.
- All teachers and instructors should be trained as agents of women's empowerment.
- Special efforts should be made by the centre and state planners and administrators to encourage participation of girls at all levels.
- National and Intrenational organisation should extend their help for the development of women education.

Conclusion

Inspite of being a developing country, we have committed ourselves to increase our efforts in the field of women's education through increased allocation but we have not been able to break the barriers between men and women. So efforts must be made to overcome all the problems of women's education in the light of the recommendations made by different committees and commissions. As result of which the government and the people of the country will have to work hard for the development of women who constitute an important segment of the society.

EMPOWERING WOMEN THROUGH EDUCATION

—Bijaylaxmi Das

Introduction

It is believed that when you educate a man, you educate an individual but when you educate a woman you educate a family. The development of a nation can not only be assured through the technological and materialistic advances, but through the quality of life. According to Aristotle, to educate means, to develop man's facilities especially his mind, so that one can acquire some political, economic, cultural and socio-economic status in the society. Education has been recognized as a major instrument for vertical mobility and help in equalizing status among different social strata. In the process of social change, education plays a very significant role. In every developing society the degree of development depends upon the degree of education system. The famous Bengali poet Rabindranath Tagore mentioned,—"If we do not spread female education, the harmony between husband and wife will be destroyed in modem educated Indian society". Thus woman's education can also bring changes in decision making and participation in every field of life.

The current framework of National Development recognizes woman as one who can play a crucial role in social reforms, economic development and also in political process. Women are the most effective providers of health care, non-formal teachers and managers of the local environment. As a wife and mother, she is the most influential member in determining the stability of her family and the development of her children's personality. Hence, the development is a pre-requisite for the all round development of the society. Education also facilitates the process of empowerment of women to fight against dowry, female foeticide infanticide, child marriage and purda system etc. The first Prime Minister Jawaharlal Nehru in his speech had highlighted the value of women education. While addressing at an Annual Conference of community development in order to awake the people he said,— "It is the women who has to be awakened. Once she is on move the household move the country moves and thus we build India for tomorrow" (Nehru, GOI Report, l958). Education is an essential process through which women are getting confidence, self-esteem and the skills to equip themselves with men. There is a famous Chinese saying, which says, If you want to plan for a year plant 'wheat', if you wish to plan for 10 years grow 'tree' but if you plan for 100 years educate your 'women'. Thus, by literacy, it does not mean that they should only read and write, but should understand various issues of life, problems and problem solving exercises. Women constitute almost half of the total population in the country. But their participation in different fields of life has been limited by the society. Even after 59 years of independence the women continue to live in a state of negligence and exploitation. India has developed several initiatives for the development of women education in national, international level.

Historical Perspectives of Women Education

The 19th century was to be watershed for women's history. The first step for women's education was established during Lord Delhousie in the year 1848-56. But it was Raja Ram Mohan Ray, the great reformer and pioneer who had tried his level best to eradicate the social evils like 'sati', 'child marriage' etc. The contribution of Iswar Chandra Vidyasagar was remarkable in the development of women status in the society. Besides these other organization like 'Brahma Samaj', Arya Samaj also work in developing the conditions of women of India. Arya Mahila Samaj founded by Pandita Prama Bai, who urged the government to give higher education to women and also stressed on training courses to make women self-reliant and economically independent.

At the beginning of 20th century a number of women movements emerged to improve and change the status of women in India. Mahatma Gandhi united a thousand of women to participate in the National Movement of Independence. This was the turning point of Indian women to be united in such a huge number for the first time. Gandhiji introduced the scheme of basic education in 1937 being realized the importance of women education. Many committees and commissions were held to suggest ways and means to spread women education. These committees and commissions are

(1) University Education Commission (1948-49),

(2) Secondary Education Commission (1952-53),

(3) National Committee on women education (1958),

(4) National Council of Woman's education,

(5) Hansa Mehta Commission (1962),

(6) Bhakta Vatsala Commission (1963), and

(7) National Committee for Women education (1970) etc.

In the year 1958 another committee was set up under the leadership of Mrs Durgabai Deshmukh as National Committee on Education especially for the education of girls at primary and secondary level. National Policy on Education (1968) emphasized on the status of women. National Policy on Education (1986), Programme of Action (1992) also reflected the education of girls and women's equality. Besides these almost all five year plans have emphasized on women's education but very little has been achieved so far after 59 years of independence. National Curriculum Framework for school education of NCERT 2000 and 2005 also stressed on making education more accessible to more number of girl both in urban and rural setting. The National Policy for the Empowerment of Women 2001 emphasized equal access to education for women and girls. The focus was particularly on girls belonging to weaker sections including the SC/ST and other backward classes/minorities.

Concept of Empowerment

Empowerment is not something which could be made available in the form of a capsule to those whom we think are need of it. Empowerment is a process which includes the following components:

- Equal access to opportunities for using society's resources.
- Prohibition of gender discrimination in thought and practice.
- Freedom from violence.
- Economic independence.
- Participation in all decision making bodies.
- Freedom of choice in matters relating to one's life.

Empowerment is not enough to provide education to women but it require a set of assets and capabilities at the individual level (such as health, education and employment) and at the collective level as the ability to organize and mobilize to take action to solve their problems. The process has to challenge both gender and social power relations. Woman is the nucleus of our civilization. She has different roles in the socio-economic status of the nation. Thus, education is a milestone for woman empowerment because it challenges the role in the present era of globalization. In the International Conference 1994, it was said that ,"Education is one of the most important means of empowering women with the knowledge, skills and self confidence necessary to participate fully in the developmental process". Women empowerment came to be associated with social justice and equality. Empowerment of women in India is intrinsically linked to their status in the society. There has been slight increase in the total female population over the years. But there is a strong preference for the son in India. The girl child faces discrimination from birth till death.

The 2001census shows that literacy rate of India is 65.38%. It is 75.85% in case of males and 54.16% in case of females. Female literacy rate has improved from 8.86% in 1951 to 54.16% in 2001. National Policy on Education (1986) and Programme of Action (1992) have given the following parameters of empowering women through education.

- Self-esteem and self confidence of women.
- A positive image of women by recognizing their contribution to the society, politics and economy.
- Developing ability to think critically.
- Foster decision making and action through collective process.
- Enabling women to make choices in areas like education, employment and health.
- Ensure equal participation in developmental process.
- Provide knowledge, information and skill for economic independence.
- Enhance access to legal literacy and information relating to their rights.

The World Education Forum (2000) made a commitment for achieving certain goals like quality education in favour of girls and women. Education provides empowerment to women in the field of social, political and economic.

Education for Social Empowerment of Women

- Women deal with education, health, nutrition, drinking water, sanitation, environment, food, shelter, science and technology for the social empowerment.
- Women access to primary, secondary and higher education has increased significantly though their % is less in administration.
- Now-a-days women in urban areas are opting for non traditional professions like administration, management, entrepreneurship, engineering, architecture, police services, army piloting etc.
- Different voluntary organizations are mobilizing the women for achieving qualitative and quantitative education for their existence.
- Education encourages the women to fight against social evils and injustice which enable them to maintain their status in the society.

Education for Political Empowerment of Women

Women have been provided the opportunity for decision making in the political field.

- Women got their right to vote in 20th century, it was in 1920 in USA, 1928 in UK and in 1944 in France.
- In 1971 the women in Switzerland got the right to vote and stand for election.
- In 1991 Lok Sabha election 7.2% of women representatives were in India. However, in the same year, women's representation has gone up 15.5% from 1990 (9.7%) in Rajya Sabha.
- In 2004 election there were only 44 women MPs in Lok Sabha.
- The women have reserved their seats in legislature, developed the leadership quality, effective participation in national and international affairs.
- Indian women has got their position as Prime Minister, Chief Minister and Governor.
- In the Panchayats and block level their position is very

encouraging.

Education for Economic Empowerment of Women

For centuries, Indian women's role has been democratic while their fathers/brothers/husbands assured the responsibility of the bread winner and protector of the family. But today women have realized that she can not remain confined in the kitchen and four walls of the home. She wants to play a multifaceted role in the socio-economic changes taking place in the society. In fact Indian women are strikingly balanced between the traditional and progressive value of the society in transition. With the development of industrial revolution science and technology the attitude of women has changed.

- Indian women have engaged themselves in different activities and professions. Nearly 100 million women are employed in the industrial sector for the social and economic development.
- The employment of women in India is the highest that is 36% of total employment in the agricultural and allied activity. This is followed by the service sector where women constitute 19.07% of total employment.
- In the industry, women comprise only 12.42% of total employed.
- In the un-organized sectors women constitute 90% of total workers.

  (80% are engaged in agriculture and allied activities and 10% in other activities.)

Conclusion

In the Rigvedic period women enjoyed a very high status in society. There were recipients of higher education and customs. During British period the prevalent custom and traditions were hurdle for social progress. Social reformers like Raja Ram Mohan Ray, Iswar Chandra Vidyasagar, Jotiba Phule, Sasipada Banarjee, Ranade and Karve advocated the spread of women education in India. In the present society the role of NGOs are very important in promoting women education because they are very close to the people and their problems. Therefore, they should provide awareness to the parents and girls to reduce the drop out rate and women illiteracy in the nation. No doubt low educational status of women in rural as well as urban areas is a stumbling block towards the empowerment of women. So it is justified that empowerment of women is possible through education. It is very encouraging that government have taken many rightful decisions for women by introducing the law against domestic violence which will protect the women from unnecessary domestic abuses.

through education. It is very encouraging that government and civil society have taken many crucial decisions and steps by introducing the new law against domestic violence which will protect the women from physical and mental violence and abuses.

INDEX